FEAR AND

FEAR AND TRUST

God-centred leadership

David Runcorn

First published in Great Britain in 2011

Society for Promoting Christian Knowledge
36 Causton Street
London SW1P 4ST
www.spckpublishing.co.uk

The author and publisher have made every effort to ensure that the external website
and email addresses included in this book are correct and up to date at the time of
going to press. The author and publisher are not responsible for the content,
quality or continuing accessibility of the sites.

Unless otherwise noted, Scripture quotations are taken from the New Revised Standard
Version of the Bible, Anglicized Edition, copyright © 1989, 1995 by the Division
of Christian Education of the National Council of the Churches of Christ
in the USA. Used by permission. All rights reserved.
Extracts from The Book of Common Prayer, the rights in which are vested
in the Crown, are reproduced by permission of the Crown's Patentee,
Cambridge University Press.

The publisher and author acknowledge with thanks permission to reproduce
extracts from the following:
'It's not that he can't speak' and 'It was beautiful' by R. S. Thomas,
from Thomas, R. S. (1993) Collected Poems 1945–1990 (London: Dent),
copyright © Kunjana Thomas 2001.
Extract from poem by Rumi: permission sought from Ecco.
Every effort has been made to seek permission to use copyright material reproduced in
this book. The publisher apologizes for those cases where permission might not have
been sought and, if notified, will formally seek permission at the earliest opportunity.

British Library Cataloguing-in-Publication Data
A catalogue record for this book is available from the British Library

ISBN 978–0–281–06389–5
eBook ISBN 978–0–281–06673–5

Typeset by Graphicraft Ltd, Hong Kong
First printed in Great Britain by Ashford Colour Press
Subsequently digitally printed in Great Britain

Produced on paper from sustainable forests

To Jackie
a God-centred leader
and to all who are calling from the walls

Contents

Acknowledgements

Many conversations contributed to the writing of this book. At one level that is perhaps inevitable, for friends know to their cost that when a book writer is in labour there are very few other topics on offer to talk about.

I am particularly grateful to those who have offered insights from their expertise in the theory and practice of leadership and in Old Testament studies. These include colleagues at St John's College, Nottingham, where I teach part time – especially Christina Baxter, David Firth, Doug Ingram and Roy McCloughry. Special thanks are due to Pauline Shelton and Carol Walker who made their own research work available to me as well as offering detailed comments on chapter drafts. Thanks also to those with whom I have shared in leadership and ministry development programmes in recent years, especially Richard Cooke, Tim Marks and Mark Pryce. I am in deep debt to many friends for their generous interest, encouragement and example – among them Bishop Robert Atwell, John Coyne, Judy Crane, Michael Mitton, David and Helen Newman, Philip Seddon, Father Silouan, Bishop Alan Smith and Chris Thorpe.

My thanks also for the unfailing inspiration of the courage and faithfulness of those I journey with in spiritual direction. Over the past year our conversations have overlapped with the unfolding themes of this book with remarkable regularity. Taking the plunge into what was an unexpected writing project was not easy but on confessing my hesitancy to my friend and work consultant Alison White I was firmly told I should write this book 'as an act of obedience'! Working with Simon Kingston and Alison Barr at SPCK has once again been a delight. Few

writers can be so fortunate in having such unfailing encouragement and professional attentiveness.

Finally, love and thanks to my wife Jackie Searle for reading
and supporting as wisely as always and who, with Josh and
Simeon, had endured once again the presence of a preoccupied
author in the home.

1

Surviving leaders

On a journey beyond certainty

―――――・●・――――

Questions that do not have an answer need to be asked very slowly.   Ann Michaels

What were we doing before we discovered 'leadership'? Does anyone remember? The questions surfaced as I drove away from yet another training event devoted to the subject.

'Leadership' is now at the top of the agenda of organizations and businesses. Type the word into any internet search engine and you will see what I mean. Advisers, consultants and training courses are everywhere. 'Leadership studies' feature prominently in the curriculum of education establishments, while in the Church, no region or denomination is now without its own 'leadership course'. We are probably close to initiative overload, but I, for one, am very grateful. As a consultant and trainer, I have benefited significantly from this awakening of interest!

Brave and creative though much of the thinking is, deep anxieties are evident too. There is talk of a 'crisis of leadership' in our world, partly because it is so easy to feel let down by those we choose to lead us when answers to urgent questions prove elusive. And an obsessive focus on 'leaders' can have a debilitating effect upon those working with or under them. When I talk to people in the worlds of local government, health care, education, national charities and the Church, I know that many are feeling bruised by the way organizational change is being managed. Driving for results or struggling for survival can have a demoralizing impact upon even the most resource-ful people.

Then again, the burden of expectation upon leaders is huge. I also listen to people who are working bravely and imagina-tively to offer leadership in communities and organizations, but who are experiencing significant resistance, frustrating pat-terns of dependency and unwillingness to take responsibility. *Being led* is as much of an issue in our context as leading – possibly more so.

Of course, every generation faces its own challenges and these are thoroughly testing times – economically, socially and spiritually. But why now the focus on leadership? How did we come to believe that this is what we need?

When life is confusing, language can help give the impression of control: 'When we give a thing a name we imagine we have got hold of it' (Lane 1998: 62). In the Church of England, for example, the shift to 'leadership' from more traditional role descriptions coincided with the hugely exciting but deeply divisive decision to ordain women as priests. Whatever the intention, at the very moment that women began to minister in full priestly partnership, the task was renamed and the focus redefined by a noun borrowed from organizational worlds habitually dominated by men.

Leadership theorists have long observed how Western ap-proaches to leadership, both secular and spiritual, are essentially 'heroic' in mode: great men (and just occasionally women) rise to the fore in times of crisis. They inspire, solve the 'prob-lem' and achieve goals on behalf of everyone else. But note that 'heroic leadership', by definition, *requires* everyone else to be helpless. 'At its heart the traditional view of leadership is based on assumptions of people's powerlessness, their lack of personal vision and inability to master the forces of change, deficits which can be remedied only by a few great leaders' (Nirenberg 1993: 340). Leader and led exist here in a thoroughly unhealthy co-dependent relationship.

More recent studies on leadership, including those exploring gender and leadership, have been asking what *post*-heroic leadership might look like. Here the focus shifts to what is found within, and is expressive of, the whole community, rather than on something imported from outside. The talk is of 'shared leadership', 'leadership in community', 'servant leadership', and communities are seen as 'leader-full' – as relational, communal, non-directive, collaborative and negotiated in style.

These insights feature in the more reflective approaches to leadership training around the country, though there is still much frustration at how slow senior leadership styles are to move away from a hierarchy/patronage model. While the Church of England's approach has been changing, it may be that an institution that has traditionally chosen its senior leaders through a secretive system it calls 'preferment' will always struggle with the consultative, collaborative transparency that post-heroic leadership aspires to.

This book began to come together when I was invited to run some workshops on the Bible and leadership. I said 'yes', but in all honesty I was weary of the subject and not convinced about the way that the Bible was commonly used in addressing it. Seeking a fresh way in, I leafed through parts of the Old Testament and found myself unexpectedly gripped by the account of a defining period in the history of ancient Israel. It tells of a people journeying from a tribal confederacy, with fierce and distinctive loyalties, to the beginning of a monarchy and the struggle to grow into one nation under king and God.

What a remarkable amount the story of 1 and 2 Samuel has in common with our own! We too are in transition from long familiar securities, and going through considerable social upheaval. We too have a preoccupation with 'leadership' as a way of securing the future. Driven by similar concerns, the elders of Israel decide that what they need is a king like the nations around them (1 Sam. 8.4–5). It is a strategy that brings its successes for Israel but it also results in some catastrophic failures and violent unrest. Like our times, theirs were marked by hope and despair, faith and doubt, loyalty and betrayal.

We struggle with the place of God in our midst, but it was no easier to do faith or theology in ancient Israel. Men, women and communities were endeavouring to find meaning in the complex stories shaping their destiny then, as we are now.

Both worlds are affected by the uneven partnership of women and men in a patriarchal society. Ancient Israel is, of course, the more conservative in this respect. How startling then to find that as 1 and 2 Samuel unfolds, it is again and again the initiative, wisdom or simply the presence of a woman that confronts or changes the prevailing script and opens the story to new possibilities – though always at a cost. As John Bell (1996) observes, 'When it comes to chauvinism, to the procuring of women for sexual purposes, to unbridled male power and to biased reporting of events in favour of men, the Bible is as good a source as any.' For its time, 1 and 2 Samuel is very subversive literature.

But what makes this text so significant is not so much the story it tells as *the way it tells it*. Nations at this time tended to cast their history in the form of epic poems. But here we find *post-heroic storytelling* – honest, subtle, non-triumphalist and undefensive. The Old Testament theologian Walter Brueggemann calls this kind of text 'survival literature' because by abandoning familiar ways of relating and describing what is going on, it becomes a subversive story with the capacity to liberate. It frees us to imagine ourselves, our own life and meaning, in radically new and adventurous ways.

Who first transcribed 1 and 2 Samuel is not known. It is highly probable that the earliest versions were written soon after the time of King David (approximately tenth century BCE). However, it has clearly gone through a number of revisions and evolved in the telling, even during the time of exile after the destruction of Jerusalem, and the mass deportations to Babylon nearly 400 years later. Somewhere in the process it became too long to go on one scroll – hence its two-volume format. Though the completion of the 'official' Hebrew text (called the Masoretic text) dates from between the seventh and tenth centuries CE, an earlier complete version exists, and extracts found among the Dead Sea scrolls appear to draw on even earlier texts which have not survived. The English Bible versions (themselves a matter of bewildering choice) are based not only on these Hebrew texts but on a wide variety of sources in Greek, Latin, Syriac and Jewish Aramaic. Reading the Bible is a highly exploratory art, and translation, like history, involves interpretation.

My approach in this book is to quote, unless otherwise stated, from the New Revised Standard Version (NRSV), one of the most reliable of the modern English Bible translations. For a more lively paraphrase, readers might try *The Message* (2007), which does not assume much knowledge of the original Bible text. When relating a story or incident I have tried to provide enough detail to set the scene and background, and I regularly give chapter and verse references in brackets (but please feel free to ignore these if they are a distraction).

Storytelling in any culture is a very precise art. In the ancient world, stories were originally spoken not written, and the sound of the words and their repetition is important. This is easily lost in translation, so where an important play on words seems to have been missed or has not been spelled out in the NRSV, I have used Robert Alter's translation in his *The David Story* (1999) as an alternative. The bracketed Bible reference is followed by 'Alter', for example, '1 Sam. 3.14, Alter'.

A different kind of storytelling invites us to adopt different ways of listening to Scripture. Christian communities find the attraction of the 'heroic' hard to resist and this colours how the Bible is heard and preached. We come expecting something directive and well defined. But storytelling in the Bible tends to 'show' rather than 'tell' us things. It *presents* rather than *expounds* or *declares* a story. So events happen, people (and God) do things, but the drama is very sparing about their motives and feelings. You have to work these out through their words and deeds (Goldingay 2000: 132). Rather like an open theatre production that relies on audience participation, storytelling in the Bible requires communal reading and exploration.

The narrator of 1 and 2 Samuel certainly encourages us to become involved. He seems comfortable to be speaking of deep matters, of things that will take time to consider and that may not provide the answers we think we most need. He appears to be remarkably free of any obligation to explain or resolve issues raised by events or to persuade us of the rightness of a particular point of view. As he weaves his narrative, he often draws on conflicting sources, without attempting to reconcile them. Politics, personality, power and theology are all factors in this story of a society journeying unevenly through change. The style is more often contemplative than didactic, reflective than prescriptive, participative than directive. It is even playful at times and the narrator has a teasing way of making comments that could be taken one of a number of ways. The listener is often left wondering quite what to make of things. Events sometimes jump out of chronological sequence without explanation, while the length of any particular story is not necessarily a clue to its significance. Very often the drama turns on a brief appearance or the action or words of an unnamed character in the wings. All in all, it does indeed feel more like joining in a lively conversation than reading the Bible!

What a contrast to the preached and 'taught' approaches to Bible storytelling familiar in many churches. The assumption tends to be made that something authoritative must be directive. But to claim that 'the Bible teaches . . .' also requires us to ask *in what way* it teaches.

I was reflecting on this as I spoke at the Lee Abbey centre in north Devon one holiday week. After each address I invited any who wished to talk further to meet me in the library, and an unexpectedly large number came each day. They were a very mixed group, and included a number of people who had given up a once lively Christian commitment. Rather than adopt a question-and-answer format, I kept passing their ideas and insights back into the group. A conversation developed that was marked by high levels of honesty and a willingness to listen and respond to very varied insights. We circled around the biblical texts, weaving our own stories in and out of them: we were often more alive in the questions than the 'answers', and for many, those conversations became the highlight of the week. They felt like an experience of community doing theology through storytelling – the stories of the Bible and our own. Faith grew afresh for some and in others was awakened for the first time.

I have found the work of psychologist James Fowler very helpful in reflecting on the different ways people and groups tell their faith stories in the changing contexts they find themselves in. What interested him was not *what* we believe but *how*, and of his six stages of faith development, two have particular relevance for this discussion (see Runcorn 2011: 109ff. for a fuller summary).

The first, which Fowler locates most commonly in early adulthood but may continue well into later life, has been called the 'tribal' or 'loyalist'. It is characterized by loyalty to given ways of believing, and faith communities of this type tend to be gatherings of the 'like-minded'. The tribal stage has many impressive qualities: beliefs and values are deeply held and levels of commitment impressive. Allegiance is to external authorities – 'the leader', the Bible, 'the organization' or 'The Party'. Leadership in such communities tends towards the authoritative, directive and functionally non-consultative. Teaching styles will favour the directive and prescriptive. Right and wrong will be sharply defined, choices clear. Those at the tribal stage will be drawn to the heroic.

In anxious or chaotic times there are powerful attractions in tribal faith. But because it is so tightly bounded and defined, it is not good at responding creatively to significantly changing environments. It tends to lack the reflective depth and flexibility needed to cope with the challenges of *long-term* transformation and can be very defensive and aggressive under threat. Paul Virilio, the author of *Speed and Politics*, could be describing tribal behaviour when he observes that a great deal of the organizational response to crisis and corporate anxiety in our time is coercive and even violent in its approach. It attempts to achieve change 'by the exercise of power' (Brewin 2004: 6), to go for pragmatic, short-term solutions that lack the depth needed to engage with the sheer complexity of the task. Similar tendencies may be evident in approaches to church strategy.

The other stage has been called 'critic' and 'reflective', which as the names imply is a thoughtful and questioning stage. It may be triggered at any time (though mid-life is particularly common) by a crisis of some sort that shatters the sense of security we may have had regarding our beliefs, causing us to lose our tribal certainties and question previous convictions. Discovering to our cost that truth is more complex than we first thought, we will feel the need to move away from a world in which life is promised and faith and God come with some kind of guarantees. This can be a painful, lonely and bewildering stage to enter. It is a kind of exile.

On the positive side, the reflective critic approach can be spacious and exploratory, open to questions without demanding answers. Those at this stage will develop the capacity to hold together diverse views, to live with contradiction and to weave together the ever-transitional stories of life. They will be drawn to mystery. To a tribal/loyalist community this can look very individualistic, but the reflective critic has come to own faith or life for herself and having done so will be able to contribute richly to quite new patterns of belonging and believing.

Though often read and interpreted with a tribal agenda, 1 and 2 Samuel is actually an example of reflective storytelling. It has a depth that only becomes apparent through long, slow listening. Strikingly undefended and non-campaigning, the narrative handles the volatile themes of politics, theology and personality and offers profound reflections on the remaking of a people, a faith and their world. It is storytelling by the wise and 'shows' a way of doing God, doing faith and doing history for any age or people who find themselves journeying through prolonged and uncertain transition. It actually models for us a way of leading, and of being led, and of seeking God in all.

In short, it traces the vulnerable but essential journey from fear to trust.

2

'In the beginning you weep'

Hannah and the unexpected starting place

------ ◆◆◆ ------

In the beginning you weep. The starting point for many things is grief, at the place where endings seem so absolute. One would think it should be otherwise but the pain . . . is antecedent to every new opening in our lives.　　　　Belden Lane

A woman walks into the temple. She is alone and burdened, her head bowed. She stands there in the place of worship. And now she can hold back no longer. She can endure no more. All restraint gives way and like a fierce storm her prayer pours out in a torrent of bitter pain and unrestrained weeping. 'If only you will look on the misery of your servant!' she cries.

But we have not come in quite at the start of the action. Let's go back a little.

'There was a certain man of Ramathaim, a Zuphite from the hill country of Ephraim, whose name was Elkanah son of Jeroham son of Elihu son of Tohu son of Zuph, an Ephraimite' (1 Sam. 1.1ff.). This is how the narrative of 1 and 2 Samuel initially draws us in. It is one of the greatest pieces of storytelling in the ancient world.

'There was a man'. Well, this much we might expect. Publicly at least, our world is a man's world and the male story, it appears, must always define human history. Note that while Elkanah's ancestry is formally summarized, his wives are simply named. It is then baldly stated that Peninnah has children and Hannah does not.

To long for children but remain childless in any culture or age is a pain like no other. A womb made for life-bearing is lifeless. As a woman, Hannah feels marked by her barrenness, revealed as helpless and powerless. Indeed, the likelihood is that Elkanah took a second wife because Hannah was unable to provide him with children.

We meet 'this man' (v. 3) – note that he is no longer referred to by name, indicating that he will not be at the centre of the unfolding story – who is on his private annual pilgrimage to the Sanctuary of Shiloh, the formal spiritual centre for God's people at that time. (This story comes from early in the history of Israel. The city of Jerusalem and its Temple do not yet exist.) It is only in passing that we discover that his wives are there at all, though Elkanah may be wishing that he had left them behind. His pious faith does not seem to have had a healing effect on his bitterly unhappy household. Though Peninnah has been blessed with children, she is resentful and insecure as the second wife, while Hannah's childlessness is made more unbearable by the merciless taunting she endures from her rival. And now, with Hannah on the edge of exploding with pent-up bitterness and anger, the narrator reveals that her suffering is not just at the hands of Peninnah. Her God is also against her: Yahweh* has closed her womb (1 Sam. 1.5–6).

How can Hannah be expected to worship and feast before the very God who has made her barren?

People living with pain find their own ways of managing it. Sometimes being in the company of others can be very hard. Hannah's way of coping with her anguish is to withdraw. I am reminded of a church service in which the congregation were spread around a number of prayer stations, centred on

---

* God is most often referred to in this story as 'Yahweh' which means I AM. This is the name revealed to Moses at the burning bush (see Exodus 3), and while most English Bible translations substitute the word 'the Lord' wherever Yahweh occurs, I have kept the original for its directness and immediacy. I discuss this name for God in Chapter 10.

different themes. In a side chapel, dedicated to 'loss', a young woman sat alone on the floor, bowed over in prayer and thought. At this point in time, her whole life was found in that spot. She was longing to conceive and had endured the pain of successive miscarriages.

Elkanah seeks Hannah out (1 Sam. 1.8) because he loves her, and because, as a man, he perceives that he must be central to her story. But in fact he is already on the edge of the action and struggling to understand what is happening. His first words are a string of bewildered questions. 'Why do you weep? Why do you not eat? Why is your heart sad?' Well, why doesn't he know? For all his gentleness he compounds his ignorance with a further question that is patronizing and completely self-absorbed. 'Am I not more to you than ten sons?' It is not only Peninnah who is sorely provoking Hannah! We can be so clumsy with each other's pain.

The confusion over the text about the sacrifice (1 Sam. 1.4–5), as to whether Elkanah gives the double portion at the sacrifice to Hannah (as a loving compensation) or to her rival (who has children to feed), somehow reflects his uncertain and ineffectual family leadership. (English Bible translations vary as to which interpretation they choose.)

Hannah now acts. She eats, drinks and then goes alone to pray to Yahweh – we presume, but are not told – at the temple shrine. We do know, however, that Eli the priest is sitting on the seat by the entrance to the temple.

There is a play on words here. Hebrew listeners would be aware that 'temple' can also mean 'palace' and 'seat' can mean 'throne'. Perhaps the text is stressing the seriousness of Eli's leadership as his royal priesthood begins to come under critical scrutiny. It certainly hints that whatever is beginning here in the temple will at some point move to a palace.

As Hannah prays, she weeps without restraint, pouring out her bitter grief to Yahweh. And it is to Yahweh she must bring it – for he is both her adversary and her ally. He has closed her womb and only he can choose to open it. Hannah makes a vow to dedicate a son, if granted her, to the lifelong service of Yahweh. It is true that desperate people can promise anything, but all that follows suggests that Hannah is making a remarkable offering, borne out of costly and profound faith.

Note how sharply Hannah and Eli are contrasted in this scene (1 Sam. 9–18). Hannah is praying; Eli is watching someone *else* praying. Hannah stands before Yahweh; Eli is sitting in the entrance to the court of Yahweh.

Hannah prays with raw immediacy. The language here is very strong: she is not being polite and feels no need to be. Phrases such as 'before Yahweh', 'to Yahweh', 'from Yahweh' occur ten times in relation to her praying. This is utterly *directed* faith.

Eli can't hear or sense that this is prayer at all, and like Elkanah he reveals his incomprehension through a question. Once more, Hannah must engage with a man who does not understand. But whereas Elkanah, we know, is distressed by his wife's pain, Eli shows himself to be brutally judgemental. 'How long will you make a drunken spectacle of yourself?' (1 Sam. 1.14).

'How long . . . ?' That cry is one of the most haunting phrases in the prayers of God's people. Over two-thirds of the Psalms are 'how long' prayers, full of grief, bewilderment, anger and forceful questioning. In Hebrew faith there are some things to which we must submit in loving trust, but there are others to which we must say 'no' in protest – even to God.

Lament in the Bible is closely linked to deliverance and praise. Many Psalms that start with protest and questioning end on a note of thanksgiving (for example, Ps. 22). It is not automatically so, but the psalmist's *relationship* to God and to the situation often changes. There is a quickening of hope, a deepened sense of God's goodness and often the surprise of joy.

Now Hannah, who has shown no restraint in addressing Yahweh, is polite and deferential to male, priestly authority.

(She is not the only woman to learn the hard way that if you want to be taken seriously by male 'superiors', tears are usually not a good idea.) She denies being drunk: 'Do not regard your servant as a worthless woman' (1 Sam. 1.16). The term used here is highly derogatory and suggests an utterly immoral character. It reveals the contempt that Hannah feels lies behind Eli's accusation. The irony is that Eli's own sons will justifiably be called utterly immoral characters in the next chapter (1 Sam. 2.12).

Hannah explains that she was praying out of great torment, but does not say what she was praying for. Without apology, Eli blesses her prayer. His words sound very formal alongside Hannah's raw immediacy, but then any church leader who has felt trapped by the attentions of an awkward or demanding personality knows the temptation to go on liturgical or pastoral autopilot. It is so easy to 'dispense' a prayer while looking over the shoulder for an escape route.

Eli is doing his job, but he prays blind. He has no idea *what* he is blessing, though the listeners know that he has just blessed a petition that will result in the birth of a child who will replace him and his sons as priest and prophet. And Yahweh hears his prayer.

The story moves quickly back home. Elkanah briefly takes charge again. He 'knows' his wife, in the ancient Hebrew way of speaking of sexual intimacy. (Though at another level of understanding, of course, he doesn't know her at all.) And even now the expected sequence is interrupted. Instead of 'Elkanah knew his wife Hannah, and she conceived', we read, 'Elkanah knew his wife Hannah, *and the Lord remembered her.* In due time Hannah conceived' (1 Sam. 1.19–20, my italics). The story is unmistakably centred on Hannah and Yahweh.

Samuel is born, and after he is weaned the day comes when Hannah fulfils her promise to Yahweh and brings him to

Shiloh (1 Sam. 1.24ff.). It is she who takes the initiative: Elkanah defers to her; Eli too is silent before her; even Yahweh does not direct her.

Back at the temple she greets the priest. 'I am the woman who was *poised* by you here praying to the Lord' (1 Sam. 1.26–27, Alter). Is she being mischievous describing Eli as 'beside her' as she prayed that day? 'Remember how we prayed together, Eli?' He was actually sitting over by the door and treated her with crass insensitivity. Our leadership and pastoral blunders do have a way of returning to haunt us.

That word 'poised' is so unexpected. 'Poise' usually speaks of balance, of a certain elegance and presence. Someone poised may also be ready for action or to respond to a signal – like an athlete. But by any normal measure Hannah had completely *lost* her poise that day. She looked drunk to at least one seasoned observer of festival behaviour. She was *un*balanced. Her face was wet with tears. Her body was racked with anguish. This is not usually described as poised behaviour. I remember a widow being commended for keeping her 'poise' as she stayed dry-eyed and stiffly formal through her husband's funeral.

But Hannah describes herself as 'poised'. It is very unusual to apply this word to public prayer, and we only find it used once again, when Yahweh comes in the night to speak to young Samuel in the temple. 'Yahweh came and stood *poised* and called' (1 Sam. 3.10, Alter). Not only is Hannah poised in relationship to Yahweh, her heartfelt, passionate, unrestrained, yearning 'poise' is mirrored in the poise of Yahweh!

Suddenly the camera pulls back, the vision becomes cosmic and Hannah sings (1 Sam. 2.1ff.). A story that began in the private grief of a family home is now proclaimed as a sign of a new world order. The opening of Hannah's barren womb is revealed as a prophetic sign of Yahweh's ways in all the world.

Hannah's song, like that of Mary centuries later, is one of revolution. She sings of a reversal of fortunes, of a God who raises the powerless and shatters the powerful, of the poor exalted. She prophesies the coming king.

Though Hannah's story has often been read as a kind of touching domestic prelude to the introduction of the prophet Samuel, it is actually key (as we shall see) to interpreting all that follows. In later chapters, a young shepherd boy will be raised up from among the least to become king. And at the far end of this long saga, after lurching from despotic and brutal power games to anguished prayer and repentance before Yahweh, King David will find himself, theologically and spiritually, precisely where Hannah's song begins. In 2 Samuel 22 he too sings his faith. There is, in the end, nowhere else to start from than raw need, human powerlessness, naked faith and anguished petition – before a God who hears and responds as he pleases.

Hannah's place at the beginning of this epic narrative is subversive of the prevailing social, institutional and theological powers – which, we have to note, are male. In fact, whatever story is beginning here, it is not one that the established order of things has any way of understanding. Both Elkanah and Eli remain on the outside of the action and ignorant of its significance. Both display impotence – the former through benign, ineffectual patriarchy, the latter through his undiscerning priesthood. We will soon learn – without surprise – that this impotence is matched by a spiritual barrenness in the land. 'The word of the LORD was rare in those days; visions were not widespread' (1 Sam. 3.1).

Where might our stories find echo in this unexpected mixture of prayer as protest, raw faith, costly sacrifice and bruises inflicted by the hardened unawareness of 'institutional' religion? Whatever emerges in due course out of the longing for 'leadership' that so defines that ancient world and ours, this opening story warns us that it will not be something established by powerful charismatic personalities, or political or military strategies. It starts and will end in a quite different place – led by the surprise and vulnerability of a woman's story, enabled by her initiative, revealed by her prayer and interpreted by her song.

3

'Here I am'

Samuel, listening and the tinnitus of God

It's not that he can't speak . . .
It is just that he doesn't,
or does so at times when we are not listening,
in ways we have yet to recognise as speech. R. S. Thomas

What does a world from which God has withdrawn look or feel like? How would we know? It may be just as noisy and excitable as ours – possibly even more so. Perhaps 'religion' and 'spirituality' would even thrive at such times. After all, it's not as if when we don't hear God, we hear *nothing*: more that we start to hear *everything*!

'The word of the LORD was rare in those days', says the Samuel storyteller; 'visions were not widespread' (1 Sam. 3.1). Of course, if 'God' is simply one lifestyle choice among many, the issue matters little. But for the narrator, the situation could not be more serious. The 'word of the LORD' is nothing less than the sustaining and renewing source of the world's life, and this sentence describes a state of existence perilously out of touch with life's true meaning and calling. The people of ancient Israel are deaf to what they need most. In our time, we too seem to have lost confidence in – or simply fallen out of touch with – the familiar sights, words and signs of faith.

In the third volume of Ursula Le Guin's *Earthsea Quartet* (1993) the fabric of the world has been torn deep within. The

19

consequences are not immediately apparent, and for some time little changes on the surface, but after a while rumours and stories start arriving from the remoter communities. Something is not right. There is a growing dis-ease. The ancient prayers and songs are emptying of meaning and losing their power to renew the land. Earthsea is a world governed by magi, but these mages have become so complacent about their invulnerability that they are unable to perceive the danger to the isle that is their home. An ancient paternal institution that has long exercised guardianship has in effect stopped up its ears just when it needs to listen most.

Now I have to declare a particular interest in this topic. I am hearing impaired. I wear hearing aids and also suffer from tinnitus. (No two forms of tinnitus are alike but a basic description would be 'a continuous noise in the ears'.) Ironically, a great deal of the work I do involves listening and facilitating others as they listen to each other. The difficulties are obvious and the process is rarely less than exhausting. But there is something truly sacramental about those moments when what is being offered is truly heard and received.

A few years ago I was fitted with new hearing aids. When you receive new hearing aids, you don't just hear what you want to hear louder. *Everything* is louder. The coffee mug hitting the table was like a pistol going off. The door slamming was like a high explosive. A loo flushing sounded like Niagara Falls. My aids were so sensitive that in a cinema toilet I picked up the soundtracks of most of the other films showing on site (and possibly a passing taxi radio as well). I had to learn to hear all over again – to discriminate what was important from interference, to distinguish signal from noise.

One in six of the British population now suffers significant hearing loss. A growing number also struggle with tinnitus. We speak of 'noise pollution', and the burden of aural and visual overload is highly stressful. We are deafened and confused by the noise of continuous, competing messages.

But even if we have fully functioning ears, we may fail to hear properly. *For listening is above all else the capacity to faithfully be present to another person.* Research shows that only 7 per cent of communication is verbal, while the other 93 per cent happens through body language, facial cues, the immediately surrounding environment, tone of voice and intuition. Long before any words are spoken we are listening and communicating intensely. Furthermore, if what is said is contradicted by what is unspoken, we will not trust what we hear. And this 'not trusting' will be largely unconscious: we will know that true communication is not taking place if the words we hear do not 'take flesh', do not become incarnate. Listening is a wholly lived, embodied process which requires the opening of the self and a relinquishing of control, in a hospitable environment. It is a tentative process, involving vulnerability on both sides. A great spiritual guide, Mother Mary Clare, once defined listening as 'a conscious willed action requiring alertness and vigilance, by which our whole attention is focused and controlled'.

The subtitles I need to watch television are a mixed blessing as far as real listening is concerned. They both reveal and conceal; they give me the words but separate them from the speaker. When I am reading subtitles I am not looking at the person involved and easily miss the cues and the slant of the voice that convey the real message. (Once, at a showing of an English film in a Jerusalem cinema that came with French, Hebrew and Arabic subtitles, I could scarcely see the film through the text!)

Actually, we all listen with subtitles in the sense that we never meet each other 'value free'. We bring to every encounter pre-conceived understandings, and while these may help us begin to hear and receive what we could not otherwise understand, they may also reinforce our prejudices and misconceptions and make *real* listening impossible.

The Bible is full of calls to hear, not least in the teachings of Jesus himself – 'Let anyone with ears listen!' (Matt. 11.15) – but

God often finds his people frustratingly deaf to his voice, and blind to any awareness of their own perverse behaviour. There are times when religious devotion is flourishing but God condemns it as 'trampling my courts', declaring, 'your . . . festivals my soul hates; they have become a burden to me' (Isa. 1.12–14). This is the deafness of 'religion' in the hands of the privileged, complacent and powerful who assume that they have God's favour and blessing. In return God closes his ears: 'I will not listen.' Terry Eagleton observes well when he writes, 'There is a document that records God's endless, dispiriting struggle with organized religion, known as the Bible' (2009: 8).

In E. M. Forster's novel *A Passage to India*, there is a crisis in the colony when an English woman visits a sacred cave that responds to sound with a particular echo (ou boum). She suffers an emotional breakdown there, and an Indian man is forced to take the blame. But for the woman, submissive up to now to the sheltering, institutionalized patriarchy of her world, the breakdown is the beginning of a breakthrough. 'Suddenly, at the edge of her mind, Religion appeared, poor talkative Christianity, and she knew that all its divine words from "let there be light" to "It is finished" only amounted to "boum"' (1991: 133). The echo of the cave mimics the hollowness of the entire colonial enterprise. A Christian empire which presumes itself to be at the height of its divinely ordained powers is exposed to the sound of its own emptiness.

Hearing impaired people know better than most that there is no such thing as casual listening: all real listening is deliberate, intentional. Listening requires a face to see, lips to read and a hospitable environment. It calls for a turning towards the other. The hearing impaired are constantly reminded how hard we find this. So much intended communication is offered indirectly and even concealed. It is not inappropriate that the biblical word for turning, *metanoia*, also translates as 'repent', for our struggle to listen reveals just how much we hide from each other. Turning away is one expression of a refusal to hear. But the New Testament also speaks of God turning his face to us in Christ, to save and reconcile, and the response of faith is to turn to him with unveiled faces (2 Cor. 3—4) in a mutual movement of love, service and vulnerability.

In the television series *The Big Silence* five people opted to spend time in a monastery learning silent meditation. Only one participant came with Christian faith and none had tried anything like this before. All were aware in different ways of searching for something and several had already sensed that their hectic lifestyles were a way of avoiding unresolved aspects of their own story. They found embarking on an eight-day silent retreat very hard and occasionally, the narrator told us, they 'rebelled', breaking silence and talking to each other. But in a culture like ours that bases its life around endless distraction, surely this was not so much rebellion as simply reverting to type. The real rebellion for us is to choose silence, to be still, to refuse to be other than truly, vulnerably present to ourselves and to the possibility of God. The participants in *The Big Silence* all emerged deeply changed. The silence broke through the drivenness and aridity of their lives and they discovered that before they could encounter God they had to be present to themselves. Their return to daily life revealed just how hard it is to sustain this sort of commitment at any kind of depth in our culture. Mother Mary Clare once described our present age as journeying through a 'communal dark night'. We should not be surprised, then, to find ourselves struggling. The pressures are huge and vision is scarce.

A capacity to hear the word of the Lord, involving a willingness to be present, is central to the story of Samuel. In Eli we have already met a priest on the edge, an isolated figure, lacking discernment, who completely misreads Hannah's distress before Yahweh. His is a wooden and formal religion in comparison to the passionate immediacy of her faith. He lacks the ability to be present.

In the two contrasting stories that now unfold side by side in the narrative (1 Sam. 2.11–26), we read first of Eli and his sons. Under their leadership the word of the Lord has grown scarce: a vocation has been betrayed and this will lead to decline and death. The focus then switches to the arrival of the young Samuel at the temple, as promised by Hannah, to begin his lifelong vocation 'to minister to the LORD'. He will learn to hear Yahweh's voice, and through him the word of the Lord will again sustain and guide his people.

In contrast to the reference to Samuel, which is brief and factual, the corruption of the sons of Eli is now described in detail. Their abuse of the pilgrims has clearly been going on for some time and 'in the sight of the LORD', and it is stated that they 'did not know the LORD' (1 Sam. 2.12, Alter). But Eli is silent.

Back to Samuel who, visited and freshly robed each year by his mother, is still 'ministering before the LORD'. Eli may be his guardian but Samuel is spoken of only in direct relation to Yahweh. He may live in Eli's house but he is growing up 'in the presence of the LORD' (2.21). Eli is credited with no influence in Samuel's development.

Only now when Eli is 'very old' does he hear of his sons' sins – the list of which is growing to include sexual promiscuity (1 Sam. 2.22). We get the impression of someone out of sight and sound of what is really happening, and his attempt to remonstrate is too little too late and pathetically ineffectual. The fate of the house of Eli is revealed by a nameless visitor who prophesies Eli's replacement as priest and the death of his sons. Eli is condemned for exploiting his privileged place as priest of the people and while we are not told any details, his sons, it appears, have only been copying his example.

Samuel is to be found steadily 'ministering before the LORD' (1 Sam. 2.18). And now, at the heart of this story, the narrator pronounces his verdict: 'The word of the LORD was rare in those days; visions were not widespread' (1 Sam. 3.1.)

And where is the priest? Eli's sight is 'dim' and he is lying down in his room, his physical decline and blindness mirroring the decline of his leadership and faith. Samuel meanwhile is lying down 'in the temple of the LORD'. The storyteller adds a hopeful detail: 'the lamp of God had not yet gone out' (1 Sam. 3.3). These are dark times, but the light of Yahweh's presence is not wholly extinguished.

And after long silence, Yahweh speaks. He calls Samuel in the night. 'Here I am', says Samuel. The boy's first words completely define his character and ministry. He will be utterly present to Yahweh and his people all his life.

There is one last change between Eli and Samuel to come. Under Eli the word of the Lord had grown scarce. Now he himself hears the word of the Lord from Samuel. It is word of his own fate and he accepts it. There is more to grieve over than to remonstrate about in a vocation lost or misused.

Samuel continues to grow for 'the LORD was with him'. The word so rare is now being spoken again through Samuel 'to all Israel' (1 Sam. 4.1). A new era has begun, under new leadership.

'Here I am' is simple to say, truly hard to mean. But no real growing, maturing or listening can take place until we are present; no meeting with God can happen if we have not really turned up! Perhaps the primary task of a leader is to be present, but it is very hard to do. (I notice this again and again in the work of spiritual direction. There are times when to come to God in prayer requires a long journey back from the far country of multiple distractions and anxieties.)

We may now have an insight into the cost of Samuel's 'Here I am'. It is far more than the chirpy enthusiasm of a youthful volunteer, but rather a personal mission statement that holds him to lifelong, disciplined attentiveness. Leadership that renews must always be 'present' to God and the people.

During one of those periods when tinnitus was wearing me down, I was sitting with a wise guide, telling of my frustrations.

I said my only sense of God's response to my prayers for relief was that my affliction would in some way become a song – a thought I had not actually articulated aloud before.

'I know what it is,' he replied immediately, 'it is an "ison".' In ancient Byzantine worship the ison is the continuous bass note held in the background by the choir. The cantors improvise and weave the worship and prayers of the church and world around it. Theologically the ison represents the sound of God – the divine song that holds all creation in being, makes all other songs possible and gives them their freedom and extraordinary diversity. The German theologian Dietrich Bonhoeffer called it the 'cantus firmus'. Writing within the darkness and turmoil of Nazi Germany, he urged his friends, 'Do not fear. Pin your faith in the cantus firmus' (Alves 1990: 8).

So my own struggle with deafness has become a kind of commentary on the continued challenges of living and believing in times like ours. If life is to have any nurturing depth and meaning, the ability to distinguish signal from noise is the biggest challenge we face. That requires that we learn to be truly present to ourselves, to our world and to God. And the thought that the very thing we wish most to be rid of – that we can only react to as a distraction that distorts what we think *really* needs saying and hearing – is actually the song that will yet save us all, is both disturbing but endlessly hopeful.

'Speak, Lord, for your servant is listening' (1 Sam. 3.9).

4

On the perils of conscripting God

Religion, theology and technology

——————•◆•——————

When anxiety reaches certain thresholds . . . even the most
learned ideas can begin to function as superstitions.

Edwin Friedman

The last chapter began in a world in which God was almost
silent. Then a young prophet heard the voice of Yahweh in the
night, and though no one but Samuel recognized or knew how
to respond to this voice, God began to reach 'all Israel' through
him. As 1 Samuel 3 ends, the language is lyrical and the mood
hopeful. A people, united in faith, are being attentive to godly,
settled leadership. The future looks good.

But now the scene changes abruptly (1 Sam. 4.1b) – in fact,
it feels as if we have mistakenly turned two pages at once! The
fact is that ancient storytelling often differs in style from contemporary narratives. Whereas we generally expect our stories
to connect up as they unfold, Hebrew storytellers sometimes
place two episodes side by side without making any explicit
connection. The listener is then invited to explore why this
might be.

Without warning, Samuel has vanished and we find ourselves
in a very different place and time. 'In those days the Philistines
mustered for war against Israel, and Israel went out to battle
against them' (1 Sam. 4.1b). In *which* days exactly? And more
to the point, where are Yahweh and his word? We seem to be
back in a world in which both are absent.

This is the first time the Philistines have appeared, and from this point on they will embody all that threatens the security and peace of God's people through this period of history. There are already clues that a crisis is looming, for the story tells us that while Israel simply 'went out to battle', the Philistines 'drew up their lines' and were 'deployed' (1 Sam. 4.2, Alter). The Israelites look unprepared and leaderless in comparison, and sure enough they are heavily defeated.

The Israelite elders discuss what went wrong. Now at any significant point in life asking the right question is always more important than finding the answer. And the question the elders ask is very significant. It is, 'Why has *Yahweh* routed us today before the Philistines?' (1 Sam. 4.3, Alter), rather than, 'Why did the Philistines overpower us?' Yahweh, their God, has defeated them, in the presence of (and with the assistance of?) the Philistines, and their business is with him. The crisis is theological above all else. But the question is left hanging: no waiting or listening follows; no prayers are offered, no sacrifice made. Yahweh is not consulted at all. Israel's God is actually and effectively absent from this whole saga.

An answer is needed – and quickly – so the question is simply abandoned and a decision made: 'Let us take to us from Shiloh the Ark of the Covenant of Yahweh that it may come into our midst and deliver us from the hands of our enemies' (1 Sam. 4.3, Alter).

On the face of it, the Israelite elders show a sound instinct in turning to the Ark. This was a large box made of acacia wood to specifications given to Moses in Exodus 25. On the top of the box were two cherubim whose outstretched wings formed the 'mercy seat' for Yahweh, and inside were the stone tablets engraved with the ten commandments, revealed by Yahweh to Moses on Mount Sinai, after the exodus from Egypt. In short, the Ark functioned as a physical custodian of all Israel's history and faith: it held their whole community memory of failure and success.

One of the most insistent challenges in the Bible is to 'remember'. If a community or organization is to respond wisely to the challenges of the present and find vision for its future, it must be in living relationship with its past. All renewal is first of all a work of remembrance, and this is never more vital than in times of uncertainty and crisis.

But the elders do not turn to the Ark to remember. The text says 'Let us take to *us*' (1 Sam. 4.3, Alter), in words that are key to interpreting all that follows. The elders simply bypass Yahweh, take charge themselves, and reduce the Ark – which is primarily a gift to recall God's people to the profoundest truths of their existence – to a cultic relic supposedly charged with divine powers. The holiest sign of God's ways is downgraded to a useful instrument. Faith is reduced to superstition. The Ark of the Lord of Hosts becomes a conscript in the Israelite army.

On the surface, this strategy possibly looked very pious. What greater sign could there be of the Israelites' seriousness? Fetched from its home at Shiloh, the 'Ark of the Covenant of the Lord of Hosts who is enthroned on the cherubim' duly arrives on the battlefield (its full formal title used to give added weight to its significance). The storyteller does name Eli's sons as its guardians, which is rather troubling, but even so, the impact of the Ark's arrival is huge. There is no denying its power to motivate and inspire. God's people shout so loud that the whole earth shakes (1 Sam. 4.5) and the Philistines are terrified. They rightly link the presence of the Ark to the memory of God's epic deliverance of Israel from slavery in Egypt, and wonder aloud if they are going to go the same way as Pharaoh's army. But instead of collapsing, they fight with the desperation of people who have nothing to lose. (Curiously, it is the character of the Philistines that is stressed in this battle. The Israelites remain strangely featureless.) The Philistines win again, inflicting massive losses and capturing land and towns. As prophesied, the sons of Eli are killed. And worst of all, the Ark is captured.

A story that began somewhere in actual history now unfolds in a mixture of legend, tragedy and pure farce. The captured Ark is taken to the house of Dagon, the Philistines' god (1 Sam. 5.2f.). In the morning the statue of Dagon is lying face down. He is propped upright again. Next day he is not only face down again but also dismembered. Worse is to come. Some kind of deadly plague breaks out – possibly a strain of bubonic plague, which offers an explanation for the otherwise unclear references to tumours and mice (1 Sam. 6.4) – and this seems to revive memories of the plagues of Egypt. The Philistines may have captured the Ark but they are in no doubt as to its dangerous powers.

With growing desperation, the Ark is moved from town to town but wherever it goes the 'heavy hand' of God strikes pitilessly and there is total panic. God is acting like a grumpy tribal deity lashing out at enemy and ally alike. The destruction continues even after the Ark is returned by the Philistines to the Israelites: they do not know where to keep it safely either (1 Sam. 6.19ff.)! Shiloh has been destroyed. But finally, the Ark is taken to a hill-top village, where it will rest for the next 20 years, and without explanation, the carnage ceases and all goes quiet.

This strange cartoon-like saga functions as a kind of satire on certain ways of trying to 'do God' and exposes these ways as presumptuous folly. It would be easy to feel from our 'superior' vantage point in history that such 'primitive' behaviour is beyond us. But it is not only ancient people who are prone to treating symbols or ideas as if they are magically charged and will guarantee certain outcomes. In a technological society that presumes its right to 'know' and is solution-driven in the face of problems, we constantly 'take to *us*' whatever we feel we need and assume it is our right to do so. Therapist and business consultant Edwin Friedman wisely observes:

> It is important to keep in mind when comparing the sophisticated-appearing understandings of our day with

the naïve-appearing of the medieval [or ancient] world, that just because an idea is sophisticated does not prevent it from functioning as a superstition when encompassing emotional processes put it to their regressive service.

(2007: 34)

Perhaps it is the way a crisis catches us unprepared and therefore undefended that allows it to lay bare our most basic default responses and beliefs. Experience suggests that it is hard to predict how we will behave at such times. Individuals with apparently few resources may reveal hitherto unrecognized depths of faith and resilience, while others who have always been outwardly strong and confident believers may struggle desperately in the face of chaos.

The Israelites' response to the Philistine threat, though seemingly sound, is to abandon faith and theology and put their trust in technology. The Ark may be seen to represent whatever we conscript to fight our battles, to achieve our ends, to guarantee victory and vindication. Some 'arks', now as then, may look very spiritual. The business and church markets alike are awash with techniques and 'solutions', none of them wrong in themselves, and some indeed brave, creative and necessary. In faith communities, one ark is often expressed as a call 'back to' something: it may be back to the Bible, back to a particular expression of faith or tradition, or back to certain moral or doctrinal 'certainties' which we are deemed to have strayed from. Now this is fine as long as we don't neglect to put in the critical thinking that our particular situation needs and simply rely on highly conservative pre-packaged assumptions. In the face of the present global financial crisis, the continuing struggles in Libya and Afghanistan and the fight against global terrorism, it is quite apparent that Western governments are no longer sure quite what ark to summon up to the battlefield. Ideological and messianic assumptions about Western (and 'Christian'?) democracy and free market capitalism have guaranteed no victorious outcome.

The point is that when symbols and strategies are separated from faith and theology, our preoccupations with status and power, with alleviating human anxieties and needs, can take over. In Israel's later history there were times when the city of Jerusalem itself, the Temple and even Yahweh's covenant with his people were assumed to guarantee divine protection. What this story warns is the deadly way in which such responses may become an effective denial of faith and an avoidance of trust in God.

As if to underline just how separated his people have become from their actual faith, it is on the lips of the Philistines that we find the only prayer in this story. As terror engulfs them their cry goes 'up to heaven' (1 Sam. 5.12). And it is also the Philistines who remind the listeners of the significance of the story of the exodus (though with the degree of confusion of detail sometimes found among people telling faith stories other than their own). As the Ark arrives on the battlefield they cry out, 'These are the gods who struck the Egyptians with every sort of plague in the wilderness' (1 Sam. 4.8).

In a curious way perhaps, the havoc that engulfs both Israel and the Philistines stems from attempts by both nations to appropriate and misuse God for their own ends. Israel tries to coerce God into acting for them; the Philistines, once things start going terribly wrong, make the 'hostile' God a scapegoat for their ills.

The storyteller wants us to make one further connection. Back at the Shrine of Shiloh, blind old Eli anxiously waits for news of the battle. In a story desperately needing initiative and movement, he is sitting (as he was when Hannah stood before Yahweh) heavy and immobile with age, and his 'eyes are rigid' (1 Sam. 4.15, Alter). He embodies the barrenness of an institution without vision or flexibility, and lacking the creative energy to seek its renewal. But then he has already been told his fate and so have we. There is a terrible passivity in waiting for what you have no power to change or avoid.

Eli does not survive hearing of the capture of the Ark. The news kills him (1 Sam. 4.18). But it is another scene that is chosen to interpret these events. His daughter-in-law, who is expecting a baby, goes into labour when she hears the news, and then dies. And the tragic loss underlines the terrible outcome of this godless saga. What was intended to guarantee glory has actually resulted in the opposite. In her final moments, Eli's daughter-in-law names her child Ichabod, which means 'The glory has departed' (1 Sam. 4.21–22).

Years later, this image would be familiar to those listening to this story in far exile in Babylon. It would evoke haunting and terrible memories of the glory departing from Jerusalem as the armies of Babylon encircled the city and the Temple and destroyed both (Ezek. 10). We are meant to make this connection: there is a warning to be heeded, and lessons to be learned. Just as in the story of the Ark, Israel's real crisis when faced with the armies of Babylon was not military but rather one of theology and faith. A terminal and unaddressed incapability lies at the heart of both stories. A people reveal themselves as unable to relate to their God in anything other than utilitarian terms. God is *our* God and therefore must guard *us*, bless *us*, be here for *us*.

Old Testament theologian Walter Brueggemann makes tough comparisons with the assumptions that drive Western society today (1986: chs 3 and 4). In consumer culture everything is an object. Everything is defined by its usefulness and what it can do for *me*. The Church, too, struggling to find ways of sustaining and renewing its life, is intensely vulnerable to this mindset. Our strategies, programmes and resources become the way we solve the problem and the God in whose name we are doing all this can be curiously bypassed.

And what did God do in the crisis facing Israel at the exile? He refused to be useful. He refused to be defined in terms of his people's need of him. The deepest crisis they faced was not that of invading armies but the departure of God.

That God may abandon his people or world is a terrifying thought. But, in truth, God's freedom to walk out is precisely where hope lies. His freedom does not make God indifferent, as we might expect. To be *un*committed is a very contemporary definition of freedom and the social damage of such belief is apparent everywhere. But even where covenants and promises lie broken, God's own free nature presses him to act. By *not* having a commitment to his people or to his world, he can choose to bring something new to life out of the ruins of the old.

After all the confusion and chaos, the Ark sits quietly on the hill top. And almost as a postscript, Samuel suddenly appears, apparently fully in charge, as if he had always been part of the story, although he hadn't. He guides the people through repentance, prayer and renewed worship to a restored life in Yahweh. Without much detail or any triumphalism we are told of the Philistines' subsequent defeat. The towns and land are restored. And to mark this, Samuel raises a monument and names the place 'Ebenezer' – which means 'Thus far the LORD has helped us' (1 Sam. 7.12). It is a name that speaks of remembrance and trusting faith rather than of ideological certainty. But careful listeners may remember that this place was actually where this story started. It was at Ebenezer that Israel's army first gathered for war (1 Sam. 4.1). It was at Ebenezer that theology was abandoned for technology. They have come 'back to' the place where they started and can now recognize it for the first time. This is a remembrance that renews and lays foundation for the future.

5

On the desire to be led

Leaders as the people's dream

———•◦•———

There is usually a direct correlation between one's need and reliance upon external authority and one's lack of true inner authority.   Richard Rohr

I often start workshops on 'leadership' with a game. In quick succession, the faces of a number of well-known leaders from different spheres of public life are projected onto a screen. People are asked to call out the first words they think of when they see the faces. Gut reaction is all important.

The response is always the same. Whoever appears, you can be sure that the words will come fast and furious: 'inspiring', 'idiot', 'ambitious', 'ruthless', 'holy' – only slowing when people are too polite to call out what they really have in mind.

What the game makes clear is just how deeply and seriously invested we are in the lives of those who exercise public leadership on our behalf. We have strong expectations, hopes and requirements of those who lead us. We are forthright in our assessment of how they match up. We are very clear about who we like and who we don't. In the discussions that follow, people often express surprise at the strength and immediacy of their reactions.

Sometimes I change the photos between conferences so that the same people appear but with different facial expressions: for example, an aggressive pose is replaced with a friendly image. The choice of words alters accordingly. What this highlights is that to a significant extent, when we respond to someone's image we are not reacting to the real person at all. Rather we are projecting onto them our own image; *we are meeting ourselves.*

Anyone who has been in leadership for some time knows this only too well. Part of the cost of leading is that whatever the agreed task, it is worked out in the shadow of people's unmet needs, unexpressed anxieties, idealized hopes and ambitions. American writer John Updike once defined a leader as one who 'out of madness or goodness, volunteers to take upon themselves the woe of a people'. 'There are few so foolish,' he continues, 'hence the erratic quality of leadership in this world.'

When a community is seeking a leader, there is a great deal more at stake than just a particular job that needs doing. The community's 'spirit', its corporate character, its story will need to be discerned and ministered to if long-term transformation is to take place.

One of the most important questions to explore in the early stages of a new leadership task is: 'How does the reality of being in the job compare with what you thought you were being asked to do and be?' You may start your reply by listing factual inaccuracies in the job profile, but invariably you will move on to reflecting on issues concerning the character of the community or organization itself. One vicar speaks of feeling like someone 'required to be part of a script I had not written'. A manager tells how as she tries to lead towards goals she thought had been agreed, she feels like someone swimming through powerful and unpredictable currents of which there had been no prior sign on the surface of the community's life.

One day, back in the story of Israel, the elders of the people went to Samuel and demanded a new leader. 'You have grown old . . . Set over us a king to rule us' (1 Sam. 8. 4–5, Alter).

Blunt though it was, this was not a request made lightly. Speaking truth to power is never easy and Samuel had been a presence of towering authority for perhaps 40 or 50 years. (He is revered as a great prophet by the Jewish, Christian and Muslim faiths alike to this day.) Why tell such a man that it is time to step aside? What are the people really asking for and why?

It is important to recognize that the idea of leadership is always embedded and worked out in a particular context, within the story of a community. It does not exist as pure theory with a universal adaptor for plugging into any organization or business that needs it! Of course, there are common insights, principles and guidelines, but there is something distinctive in the expression of 'leadership' that requires detecting: it must take flesh.

Samuel is ageing. A great era is passing. The people are anxious about the future. Who will take over from him? Samuel may have been hoping that his leadership would pass to his sons, but their unsuitability seems to be apparent to everyone (1 Sam. 8.3). It is perhaps for this reason that the people request not a successor – another prophet/judge – but a kind of ruler they have never had before: a king. Sometimes an idea appeals simply because it is new and comes unburdened by the accumulated baggage of history.

The unfolding narrative of Samuel, Saul and David can only be understood as part of the people's story. It develops in response to several factors: the desires of an anxious community; rival tribal power groups; international and military unrest, and issues connected with the faith, theology and vocation of God's people. Some believe that a monarchy will help the nation find a new sense of security; others regard the request for a king as an outright rejection of Yahweh's leadership. It usurps the place of Torah (the Law of Moses) and undermines the vocation and freedom of God. Across the Scriptures generally, 'leadership' is an idea that sits in tension between the Kingship of Yahweh, his word and his people's story. As it still does today.

Israel's request for a particular kind of leadership – one that was routinely regarded as corrupt and brutally self-serving – comes as a surprise. The story tells how Samuel warns them that a king will 'take' (1 Sam. 8.10–17) – the word is repeated four times – their men, their women, their servants and their land. A king would require nothing of them except to submit, obey – and suffer. Surely this much was apparent? But what we have seen of this people and their elders suggests that they are a community from whom leadership has already 'taken' a great deal. Whatever the strengths and gifts of Samuel's leadership, his style has been highly autocratic. He clearly 'rules over' his people and under him they seem subservient, easily overpowered and highly dependent. They are told what to do and show no recorded interest in being part of any decision-making process. Is this how it was? If so, their demand for a leader is neither rational nor emotionally literate. It is rather the response of a people who have been trapped in highly dependent relationships and who do not have the will to opt for anything but more of the same.

Examples of this may be observed in regions of the UK that were strongly affected by the industrial revolution. They have often remained among the most economically disadvantaged areas. The forebears of the current population experienced factory owners, industrialists and other leaders 'taking' a great deal from them in terms of confidence and self-esteem. Experience shows that these things are not easily restored, and community workers have spoken of the struggle to identify local leaders and sustain local initiatives.

'Learned helplessness' is the psychological term for a condition in which people cease to believe that they can exercise any personal choice or initiative over their lives, and anxious and dependent communities will tend to be drawn to more authoritarian styles of leadership. They will find security in the feeling that someone is definitely in charge. But is that what would be most helpful for them? Going back to the Samuel narrative, doesn't there seem to be a conversation missing – one in which the people are helped to talk through what they are actually seeking and why? It is notable, too, that this demand for leadership is not a *theological* one. Not for the first or last time in this story, we see theology vanishing when the people's most basic securities are at issue. It will not come as a surprise that the unfolding story struggles throughout to find a theological outcome.

'Give us a king *like they have got.*' Who are *they* in our world? I suggest that *they* are any organizations, businesses or people on our borders, that seem, to our anxious eyes, to have found 'answers' to the challenges and problems we are facing. So for 'king' today read CEOs, appraisal schemes, HR, best practice, restructuring and middle managers.

This is particularly relevant to approaches to leadership and management in the Church of England. In the course of my work I have attended numerous national briefing days to launch Clergy Development Reviews – now a mandatory, annual requirement for all ministers in the Church of England. These days they are fronted by panels which always include a human resources professional from the business or banking world. The message is clear. We ('the Church') need to find new ways of doing this and 'they' ('the Business and Banking world') are the organizations and people who know how. It is worth noting that these organizations command budgets that the Church, in its capacity as an employer, could only dream of. And there are other concerns. After one such event I happened to meet with someone who worked in the bank represented at the briefing and had experienced its approach to work reviews from the inside. I learned that the process put forward as an effective tool to enable a flourishing and developing workforce had all too often felt coercive, competitive and relationally corrosive. At the time I was part of a group beginning to implement the Clergy Development Review in the diocese where I worked. Two members of the group had had long careers in the health service and business management before being ordained, while another had been involved in professional reviews in the police force. Though firmly committed to strengthening church leadership, they were strongly critical of their previous review and development experience and saw their involvement with this new review group as an opportunity to find better ways.

One of the honourable qualities of the Anglican church tradition is its willingness to draw on a wide range of sources for its learning. But this does presuppose a confident theological framework (sadly not always apparent!) within which to test, critique and respond to what we are seeing and hearing around us. A significant number of clergy now attending the many leadership development courses around the country have had previous careers in business or industry. They know very well that what they are being urged to draw on as examples of 'best practice' may in fact be 'rather mixed practice'. There is an understandable uneasiness about the Church being in thrall to and intimidated by secular business theory and language, and a lack of conviction that Christian practice and theology might actually inform this process – both secular and religious – and even transform it.

After all, wasn't Israel supposed to be a sign of a *different* way among the nations? And isn't the Church, too, called to model a *different* way of doing things?

In his classic book, *Christianity Rediscovered*, the Roman Catholic missionary Vincent Donovan told of his work with the Masai tribes of Tanzania. He had led a number of clans to faith and into the first steps of Christian discipleship, and when the time came for him to leave, he asked them what kind of leadership they wished to establish in his place. 'What will you call the one who takes my place, the one from your community who will do my job among you when I am gone?' They discussed it at length. It was a new question. They were now *God's* people, so certainly not a *laibon* (witch doctor), nor a *legwanan* (chief) –

for what role could there be for a chief among the people of Christ? Nor did they want an *olkarsis* (rich one/powerful one) or a *olkitok* (head one). They chose instead for the role someone who would be present in every community, interested in all the flocks of a tribe (not just their own), and supportive of every phase of community life. This was the *ilaretok*, the helper or servant of community (2001: 157).

How interesting, then, to find that the only passage in the Torah to mention kingship in Israel addresses the same concerns and teaches a very similar vision for community-based servant leadership. Deuteronomy 17.14–20 anticipates a time when the people will ask for a king on almost identical terms as in the Samuel story. Yahweh, it seems, is already disposed to allow the request. The passage warns against the temptation to identify leadership by outward signs of status (property, wealth or possessions). Nor is the king above the Law: a special copy of the Law must 'remain with him all the days of his life'. The vision for leadership here is non-hierarchical and collaborative, exercised among and within the community, without the leader 'exalting himself above other members of the community'.

So how might Israel's story have unfolded if Samuel had sat down with those elders, encouraged them to talk through their concerns, trusted them to be able to think through and take responsibility for their own needs, and taught faith in a way that enabled them to reflect theologically on their vocation as the people of Yahweh – a people whose values and ways are *not* those of the other nations?

There is much talk of a 'crisis of leadership' in our times and there are grounds for concern. But what may be more critical is the crisis of *community* – a collective abdication from shared responsibility and a tendency to regress into 'victim' mentality in conflict. This creates a culture of blame marked by an inability to sustain long-term commitments and a perversely ambivalent subservience to 'the powers' while projecting messianic expectations onto those appointed to 'rule over us'.

The task of developing leadership will never be effective unless it sits within the task of developing community. Until a community takes charge of its own leadership responsibilities, only certain kinds of formal leadership are possible and these may actually hinder the growing that is necessary.

6

'Selfhood begins in walking away'

Saul the undifferentiated leader

————•·•·•————

It is the tragedy of political lives that they are lived in reverse.
The moment of greatest expectation comes with the least
experience.   Anon

The old Victorian church was falling down and the congregation sold the site and built a modern church centre nearby.
Their investment took a considerable amount of money and a
great deal of faith. Coinciding with the completion of the new
building, a young vicar was appointed to take them into the
new era. John was gifted and enthusiastic but from early on,
his approach ruffled feathers and caused concern. He was, in
unsuspected ways, a very vulnerable man. The task of leading
a strong-minded community with its own hopes and dreams
proved quite beyond him, and barely a year into the job he had
a breakdown, resigned, and also left the ministry.

Talking to John during his time at the church centre, I recall
his struggle to own his fragilities and to take responsibility for
areas of his life that needed careful integration. His default
response had always been to use his enthusiasm to outrun his
fears. But he also spoke of feeling the burden of expectation
on him as a leader. The community, which held varied and
conflicting views on how things should be done, was going
through a vulnerable stage as it left behind the familiar and felt
its way into the strangeness of the new. A successful leader
would have needed the capacity to hold together powerful and

contradictory forces, something John quickly found that he lacked the strength to do.

Whenever I read the story of Saul who failed as Israel's first king, I remember John. Though there is no hiding from the seriousness of Saul's downfall, it is hard not to feel sympathy for him. 'I hope you will be kind to Saul,' said one person on hearing that I was writing this book.

The people have asked for a king and will not be put off the idea. Yahweh has agreed to give them one, and the next stage of the story now begins. 'There was a man . . .' (1 Sam. 9.1). The ancient formulaic opening returns to introduce a very prestigious family from one of the most powerful tribes of Israel. They have an incredibly tall hunk of a son called Saul – 'a fine and goodly young fellow, and no man of the Israelites was goodlier than he, head and shoulders taller than all the people' (1 Sam. 9.2, Alter). This is meant to sound over the top! And it is noticeable in these stories that whenever anyone's physical attractiveness is stressed, the outcome is not usually a happy one.

But there is something very contemporary about an approach to public leadership that focuses on looks and appearances. For all the sophistication of our interview and appointment procedures, we live in a media- and celebrity-driven culture where image is all. It is difficult to get past the 'virtual' impression to the real content. What do we make of the fact that the average American President is two inches taller than the general (male) population? Research shows that CEOs and senior executives of large organizations also tend to be taller than their counterparts. An extra inch is reckoned to be worth an additional $800 a year in salary in the American business world. Height is also assumed to be a sign of greater competence and authority: the highly successful CEO of a large American corporation laughs as she admits to wearing three-inch heels to increase her height at the office. 'It is a lot of bunk – but it works!' she says.

But back to handsome Saul, who, blithely innocent of what is to come, has walked some distance with his servant, looking for lost donkeys in the wilderness. (He might have done better looking for a job in New York.)

Saul now speaks, and in Hebrew storytelling the first words spoken by a person reveal their character. Saul's are: 'Let us turn back, or my father will stop worrying about the donkeys and worry about us' (1 Sam. 9.5). He seems to be a man continually disabled by anxieties about what others are thinking or doing. If first *actions* also disclose a person's character, then he is revealed here as a man unable to find what he is looking for. In fact, as we will see, Saul spends his life searching for what usually eludes him and struggling to achieve what he sets out to do. Little about him is decisive or constant and he relies on the initiative of others for guidance. Here in the desert, it is his servant who keeps nudging him along, and his servant who has heard that there is a holy man nearby with a reputation for guidance (1 Sam. 9.6–12). This is Samuel, the spiritual leader of God's people, of whom Saul is apparently unaware, showing alarmingly limited knowledge of the world beyond his immediate experience. Privilege is no guarantee of maturity.

Events move fast. Saul may have arrived at Samuel's house by accident but Samuel knew that he was coming and had been told by Yahweh that this young man was to become king. Samuel anoints him in secret (as David will later be anointed), emphasizing that Saul is Yahweh's sovereign choice, but adding to the unsettling undercurrents in the story so far. The need for concealment must reflect a degree of political danger in the process of transition to monarchy.

The first king of Israel returns to his family and says exactly nothing (1 Sam. 10.16)! His public coronation some while later carries secrecy to almost farcical levels. Samuel gathers the people (1 Sam. 10.20–24) and, as if no choice had yet been made, leads them through a ritual guidance process based on the casting of counters of some sort. The choice narrows down from tribe to clan to family until Saul is revealed as the chosen one. But at this point he has gone missing. Showing a curious lack of initiative, the people ask Yahweh where he is and Yahweh has to reveal that his choice of king is hiding in the baggage just behind them. Saul is hauled out. Obviously, the event needs some rescuing, and quickly. This is the moment for Samuel to declare that Saul is Yahweh's choice and to share how Yahweh has been guiding events. Instead, Samuel chooses to stress how good-looking Saul is! Theology does have a way of going missing at crucial points in this story.

One of the storyteller's methods for highlighting issues he wants us to notice is to contradict himself. We are told, 'All the people shouted, "Long live the king!"' But then it becomes clear that *all* did not: only 'warriors whose hearts God had touched' followed Saul, while other 'worthless fellows' refused to pay tribute (1 Sam. 10.24–27). The sympathy of the story-teller is with Saul here. And though Saul's kingship will end in tragedy and failure, we are given a hint of how it might have developed. Theology makes a return to the story, and despite the understandable uncertainties of the people, Yahweh is to be found working to establish his chosen king, 'touching hearts' and inspiring loyalty.

In the midst of much human hesitation, the *possibility* of Saul the king is affirmed. However, Saul's appointment remains an unconvincing one, and his reign does not get under way in any real sense until he achieves a first military victory. Fighting battles was part of what Israel was looking for in a king, so this is very good news. Samuel and the people gather again and 'renew the kingship' (1 Sam. 11.14). Saul has now been appointed three times.

Anyone involved in appointing or being appointed to significant responsibility will understand this sequence of events. An important part of the process does usually take place in secret. Even after open advertising and a competitive interview process the power to 'anoint' can still rest with one or two people who may function with little or no accountability. And when those responsible for an appointment feel that they have made God's own choice, it can be very hard to disagree. Of course, there comes a point when the leader appointed, however inspiring of appearance and even divine favour, must demonstrate an ability to do the job. We all wait and watch for the first 'success' that confirms the choice was right. And at that point we (unofficially) 'renew the appointment'.

There was a crucial moment at the beginning of this drama that is easy to miss. After Samuel had secretly anointed Saul, he dictated to the new king a detailed sequence of events that would take place in his life over the following week (1 Sam. 10.1–9). Clearly this was intended to encourage Saul that Yahweh was with him. But in a narrative usually quite sparing on detail it feels quite controlling: Saul may be king but Samuel is clearly still running the show. Saul hasn't actually said a word since being anointed.

Now, as Samuel finishes his briefing, we read, 'and it happened as he [Saul] turned his back to go off from Samuel, that God gave him another heart' (1 Sam. 10.9, Alter).

If Saul is to be a king in his own right he must turn away from Samuel's controlling presence. Samuel actually and psychologically represents 'the powers' that stand in the way of Saul's destiny. The storyteller knows what must happen if Saul is to measure up to his calling. So does Yahweh, who has inspired hearts to follow Saul. And Yahweh now gives his king the heart he needs for the task.

'Selfhood begins with a walking away,' wrote poet C. Day Lewis. Inspired by the memory of leaving his young son at the gates of a public boarding school this line offers a rather questionable (and traditionally male) understanding of selfhood as separation. But I use it here to explore a core responsibility of leadership: the letting go of things and people who, for good or ill, have been defining our sense of who we are. Leadership consultant Edwin Friedman calls this the task of 'differentiation' (2007: 183).

To differentiate is to establish the difference between things – in other words, to be capable of seeing the wood for the trees – and Friedman argues that this is the single most important task for leaders in contemporary Western culture. Our social environment is characterized by high levels of chronic anxiety and, for all its technological advance, our culture is in emotional regression. Friedman sees this problem as systemic, by which he means that it is more fundamental than a tendency to worry. Anxiety is effectively installed as society's driver, and in such a climate people will be attracted to leadership that promises to solve the problem (or save the world). But if a leader is working *within* the agenda of an emotionally dysfunctional system, he or she can only remain part of the problem.

For Friedman, leadership training that puts the emphasis on how to motivate or manipulate others is quite destructive. The important thing is to understand the significance of the leader's own presence and being for the community as a whole in emotional rather than theoretical or cognitive terms.

Differentiation allows me to establish and sustain a personal identity apart from the social system I am part of. I can only flourish and fulfil my vocational task if I am able to separate myself from, and connect to, my immediate world – in other words, to take responsibility for my own emotional well-being and destiny.

One sign that we are struggling to differentiate is when we are not sure where our own feelings end and the anxieties of the community start. The boundary is blurred. A clue may be that other people or situations (or God) keep getting in the way of the story we *want* to be telling. A differentiated leader will have the ability to tell the story *without blaming anyone else*. (It is astonishing how hard this is to do!) An undifferentiated leader, on the other hand, will probably be unaware of how many other people there are in the room (metaphorically speaking), and no memory of inviting them all in.

Anxious communities are highly infectious places. They are essentially reactive in their behaviour and tend to herd around personalities or issues, though without much consistency. They blame rather than take responsibility; they pursue quick-fix solutions and struggle to sustain the attention that longer-term work requires. These communities lack the leadership they most need – precisely because their anxiety has the effect of undermining or excluding it. The role of the differentiated leader is to be a non-anxious presence, operating outside the emotional climate of the day and thereby offering the possibility of challenging and changing the prevailing script.

Friedman was a family therapist as well as a business analyst and consultant. He found that the emotional dynamics evident in the family are essentially the same as those at work in the world of business. What happens in the boardroom is much the same as what happens in the kitchen. This helpfully challenges assumptions about 'leadership' as some kind of elite force in society. The gift of differentiated people to a family, community or workplace is that they 'function as the immune system of their world' (2007: 17).

Experience shows that it can be particularly difficult for leaders within religious institutions to function in a differentiated way. Perhaps this is because the language of love and commitment leaves little place for a positive understanding of the separation that human flourishing needs. Turning your back and walking away is not usually regarded as godly leadership! But the evidence is that many in Christian leadership wish that they could do exactly this. Research a few years ago revealed that three out of ten ministers have felt, for prolonged periods, like leaving the ministry. Seven out of ten feel consistently overburdened by the task. An estimated 200 ministers a week in the UK miss Sunday activities through stress-related issues (Lawrence 2004: 13).

It is the unexpected encounters that lay bare our vulnerabilities. Some years ago, when I was leading a lively congregation that was going through some painful conflict, I was cornered after a meeting by a church member. He shouted in my face, 'There's something very wrong at the heart of this church!' I felt that his words were a personal attack, that as I was the leader of the church there must surely be something very wrong with me. I later replayed the conversation and in a moment of graced intuition, I heard the wording reversed. He was now shouting, 'There's something very wrong at the heart of my life!' It was actually a cry for help rather an accusation. Further conversation revealed that he was a man of deep insecurities, and as the community he belonged to grew in new ways, he was finding that it no longer offered him places to hide from the challenges to his own maturity. The last thing he needed was an undifferentiated leader taking responsibility for all this! The problem needed locating where it belonged and nothing could change until that happened.

Another sign of undifferentiated leading is losing sight of ourselves in the role and demands of the job as it takes us over. 'Role ambiguity' is one term for simply not knowing what we are supposed to be doing. 'The severest test of work today is not of our strategies but of our imaginations and identities,' says work consultant and poet David Whyte. He writes:

> Our lives take the form of an absence. We become exhausted from the effort needed to sustain our waking identities. The day may be full, we may be incredibly busy, but we have forgotten who is busy and why we are busy. We lose the conversation, we lose our calling, we lose our sense of captaincy [his word for self-leadership], we have to realise that our lives are at stake . . . We must know how easy it is to forget, how easy it is to drift onto the rocks and put our lives to hazard. (2001: 60)

The wisdom teachings of all the ancient spiritual traditions have long understood this peril and have their own names for it. What Friedman calls 'differentiation' the Christian desert fathers and mothers of the fourth century called 'detachment', and Ignatius of Loyola, the founder of the Jesuits, taught as 'active indifference' (Lane 1998: 188). This is neither disinterest nor withdrawal, though an anxious community will experience it as such. It is rather a capacity to be detached and so create the free space within which transformative relationships are possible.

Leadership at any level of responsibility needs this subversive quality in relation to the prevailing powers – be they the manipulative 'needs' of the community, 'market forces', opinion polls, pressure from the board/employers/bishops or the coercive claims of techniques and strategies. There is a cost: a differentiated leader is not following 'the script' and an anxious community will resist and try to undermine such a person.

The real tragedy of Saul, the man and king, is that all this eludes him. His life never really quite begins. He never emerges as his own man at any level. Temperamentally unable to take responsibility for himself, he is only once described as happy (1 Sam. 11.15). He seems constantly out of touch and lacking the information he most needs to act, and as king his initiatives are fitful and hesitant. The journey from loose tribal federation to united monarchy would be demanding for any nation, and would require hugely experienced leadership. Saul has no experience of leadership at all.

Where he needs support he is opposed. His relationship with Samuel leaves him constantly wrong-footed, dependent, voiceless and humiliated. Unreconciled to the idea of kingship and resentful of his own rejection, Samuel effectively drives Saul to the edge of breakdown. The two men are trapped in a destructive, co-dependent relationship that will extend even beyond the grave. Nor is Saul able to cope personally or professionally with the challenge presented by David, whom he repeatedly tries to kill. A lonely figure, the only person in the whole story to offer him any degree of understanding and the warmth of human support is the witch of Endor (1 Sam. 28.21–25)! Unable to establish himself within the community he leads, Saul ends up acting out the anxious, unintegrated scripts of his people.

There is little sign that he has any nurturing relationship with his God. When he seeks Yahweh's guidance he receives no answer. At the very beginning of his reign he is 'seized' by an ecstatic experience of the Spirit. But this is not sustained, and the effect is eccentric rather than encouraging. After his rejection as king there is another prolonged ecstatic episode where Saul lies naked – a scene that symbolizes his unrobing as king (1 Sam. 10.10; 19.23–24). And these two events bracket the life of a man and king who never found a sustainable prayer of his own. Faith, too, needs differentiation.

7

How are the mighty fallen!
When leadership fails

———•·◆·•———

*We only really learn from our failures. Our successes confirm
us in our habits.*   Clive James

He just sat there sobbing uncontrollably. He was 18 months into
a job he had been unexpectedly and strongly encouraged to
apply for. It was a newly created post and he knew that it would
be a challenge, but he had accepted, believing that God was
calling him. Now, so soon, he was exhausted, bewildered, crushed
by the experience and feeling both unsupported and guilty that
he couldn't cope. There was no one he felt he could talk to about
his struggles. If his confidence had not been so low he would
have been very angry at being so misled – not least by God.

No leader chooses to fail. Leaders deserve our gratitude and
compassion, and it is very painful to watch someone sinking
in a job that is overwhelming them or to which they are simply
ill-suited.

The story of 1 and 2 Samuel is a sustained reflection on the
experience of failure. At its midpoint, where it is customary
in Bible stories to find the central message, comes David's
moving lament over the deaths of King Saul and his son
Jonathan. Three times we hear the cry, 'How the mighty have
fallen!' (2 Sam. 1.19). That anguished refrain becomes a lament
over a whole lost era.

On the surface, it all started with the people's request for
a king (though, of course, the real story began long before in

a quite different place). Israel's leadership was at a critical point, its present life failing and change clearly needed. But a king? Samuel is sent to warn the people what to expect – someone who will abuse his powers, oppress, exploit and 'take' (1 Sam. 8.11–20). So much would have been apparent if the people had simply looked over the border to neighbouring nations. 'Leadership' always comes with a health warning in this narrative and the people's determination to have a king seems misguided at least. They are attempting to solve a problem without recourse to conversation, theology or discernment. They have not thought – let alone prayed – things through, and then as now, 'what is not owned is not transforming' (Hirst 2006: 115).

It is Yahweh who makes clear the most serious implication of the request for a king. Samuel's fierce denunciation of the evils of 'kings' is followed by an even sharper divine judgement on the kind of people who ask for them in the first place. The people are casting aside their God, he says to Samuel (1 Sam. 8.7–8) – something they have done repeatedly through history. The consequences will be catastrophic. The nascent hopes and ambitions for monarchy and nationhood that Israel entertains will die in a far country in the bitterness of exile. City and Temple will be reduced to rubble.

This story undoubtedly offers material for profound reflec-tion, but just in passing, we might wonder what Samuel or Yahweh would have to say to a contemporary world so pre-occupied with organizational change and 'leadership', and strug-gling unevenly to find a sound theological basis for its vision.

From another perspective 'leadership' in this narrative is revealed to be an almost impossible task. *Every* leader in the story fails – a thought that draws wry smiles of recognition at leadership seminars. However committed we may be to developing skills and competencies, those involved in leadership cannot be unaware of its challenges. It is unrelentingly hard work, can be brutally thankless, and is never more costly than when it seeks to be godly and just. Leadership 'takes' from leaders and is not always good at giving back. It is lonely and can be very bad for your health. The church leader who does not, at least at times, find the thought of stacking shelves in the local supermarket an attractive alternative is the exception rather than the rule.

There is a Bible passage, commonly read at ordination services or at the appointing of ministers, which begins, 'For the love of Christ compels us' (2 Cor. 5.14, my translation). It goes on to insist that we must live with the perspective of Christ in all things and not judge people or situations from a human perspective. Moving and inspiring though this may be, leaders would do well to take note of the verse immediately before: 'If we are mad – it's for God!' (2 Cor. 5.13, my translation).

Are we allowed to feel sympathy for Saul? There are a few signs of compassion in the narrative. He is a lonely, hesitant character, seemingly lacking the very particular skills it would take to lead an organization or community into a significantly new vocational identity. It may well be that the expectations, tensions and hopes that were loaded onto Israel's first king would have sorely tested the abilities of the most gifted leader. Perhaps Saul was the monarchy's scapegoat?

Then again, the whole enterprise was ill-conceived. At the time of writing, a premier football club has just appointed its seventh manager in five and a half years. The new manager admits that many of his colleagues think him mad for taking the club on. A fresh face or personality, however gifted, will not be the answer while the real problem remains undiscerned. 'New blood rarely thwarts malignant processes anywhere. Indeed with both cancer and institutions, malignant cells that appear dead can often revive if they receive new nourishment' (Friedman 2007: 6).

Saul is treated even more harshly in the book of Chronicles, the other record of this history, where he is tersely referred to as one who 'died for his unfaithfulness . . . therefore the LORD put him to death' (1 Chron. 10.13–14). Perhaps that is not surprising. When any business or organization sets out to rebrand itself before the world, the choice of leader for the new era is vitally important. The stakes are very high. The world is watching. Israel specifically restructured its national leadership using a model that was meant to make it look and feel like the world around it, and things went tragically wrong. It was a very public failure.

For all the things working against Saul – including being professionally under-resourced for the job and clearly under-mined by those whose task it was to offer help (Samuel frequently questions or criticizes him) – notice that throughout the story he is treated as responsible and accountable. We are a long way from a contemporary victim and blame culture here. Saul's own freedom and selfhood is honoured, and for all the signs of his hesitancy, there is a strand in the narrative that suggests that Yahweh never lost belief that Saul's reign could have succeeded. Then as now, the primary vocation, and perhaps the hardest to be faithful to, was the way of radical, naked trust in Yahweh. No amount of training and strategy could substitute for that.

Saul's downfall was a failure to trust and obey. Yahweh says that he has 'turned back' from doing his will (1 Sam. 15.11). We first met Saul as he turned back without finding lost donkeys in the wilderness. He needed to turn his back on Samuel in order to take to heart the role of king. In the end, the task of 'turning' both defines and eludes him.

Not everyone fulfils their potential, but it may be that what really matters in the end is to have the courage to fight our fear of failure, to learn, to explore and to take the risks we need to in order to grow. We live in a culture that instils a terror of failure, and that is very unhealthy.

Judy Hirst tells the story of a high-achieving businesswoman and committed Christian whose career path had been moving steadily upward. By any measure she was very successful, but for reasons that never became clear her career stalled. Suddenly she was *not* being promoted or head-hunted. Hirst notes how traumatized her friend was by this. An able and confident woman was now having crises of confidence and self-worth. Why? 'Failure' exposed the woman to the degree to which her identity was based on the illusion of 'success'. Hirst continues, 'Failure can free us from illusion and help us to take a good long look at our reality. It can help us to find out who we really are. Something many of us, especially successful people, never do. If nothing else failure can potentially free us from ourselves.' For her friend, 'failure exposed her success for what it was: a huge distraction from the getting on with the real business of life which is learning to live in the grace of God' (Hirst 2006: 109).

After a long, faithful and successful ministry Samuel too had to face failure. His leadership was rejected by the people. There is no minimizing how painful this must have been. His whole life could be defined by his first words, 'Here I am' (1 Sam. 3.6), revealing a man totally available to God as his people's judge and prophet. If the challenge to Saul was how to make a beginning, for Samuel it was about how to manage an ending.

In recent years two old men have featured prominently in film and popular literature. Gandalf, the wizard in *The Lord of the Rings*, and Professor Dumbledore, headmaster of the school for wizards in the Harry Potter stories, embody many qualities that we might aspire to in our later years. Both bring the gifts of widely lived and well-processed experience. Both are significant mentors and guides to younger characters. Both have taken time and trouble to enter and understand worlds very different from their own (a quality dismissed as eccentric or irrelevant by some of their peers). Both are able to function peaceably without being the centre of the action. Both display a combination of gentleness and decisiveness, authority and compassion. Both are reconciled to their own dispensability and accept that when the time comes, the world will continue without them.

If we judged Samuel by any of these measures of leadership, he would fail significantly. A hard and inflexible character, he is clearly embittered by his rejection as leader and unable to accept the failings of his own family as the reason for this. He is unreconciled to the establishing of a monarchy even though Yahweh has agreed to Israel's request, and unable to be any kind of support and mentor to Saul. He could have been a wise counsellor in the court of the new, but instead he effectively undermines the hesitant young King Saul, appearing to trip him up whenever Saul tries to take the initiative. Samuel's arrival days later than agreed, while Saul watches his army reduced by half through desertion in the face of a powerful enemy, is one key example (1 Sam. 13.8–10). When Saul finally takes action and offers the sacrifice that Samuel was coming to make, Samuel announces Yahweh's judgement on the king even though the issue was his own lateness.

After Saul's coronation, Samuel uses his retirement speech to launch an entirely uncritical defence of his own ministry and, with Saul beside him, harangues the people for their 'wickedness' in demanding a king. He leaves them terrified by his bullying rhetoric and power play. 'All the people greatly feared Yahweh and Samuel,' says the storyteller, and you are left wondering who they fear more (1 Sam. 12.18).

Simon Walker suggests that the main task of leadership is to 'enable people to take responsibility . . . the task of enabling people to move towards fully mature, responsible personhood. Leadership is a way of offering life to the world, in order to draw life out of the world.' This means that a vital quality in a leader must be the ability to *relinquish* power. Only then may others enter theirs. 'Unless they can let go, leadership will always be an exercise in self preservation' (Walker 2007–08: 153–7).

In this respect, too, Samuel fails. His years as leader have left his people dependent and lacking initiative, clearly living in fear of him. Some readers of this story have suggested that Saul was actually Samuel's choice as king, procured through the pretence of divine guidance. If Samuel was seeking a puppet ruler he could control, that would explain his rage when Yahweh announces that he no longer wants Saul as king (Alter 1999: 73). We might note the way in which Yahweh's voice and Samuel's voice are interchanged in the story, and how the narrator leaves open the question as to whether, at times, Samuel knows the difference. Faithful though he has been, he comes over as a man hardened by the burden he has carried. It is at least possible that Samuel was not aware of how possessive he was about his role and status. He lacked the emotional literacy to see that he could only relate to other leaders in terms of his control and influence over them and was inclined, possibly to a fatal degree, to regard them as rivals.

Institutional leadership today faces similar challenges and temptations when change is in the offing. It needs to display grace in surrendering control and a willingness to open up space for something as yet unknown to unfold.

When Simon Parke's life had to take a completely new direction, he worked hard to establish himself as a writer. Here, in a newspaper article, he describes his reaction to yet another rejection slip from a publisher and goes on to offer a wise reflection on the challenge of facing failure without bitterness. There are, he observes, two different ways of managing rejection.

> I gratefully recognise the chasm between resignation and surrender. Resignation is the angry admission that I cannot get my own way; surrender is the peaceful acceptance that 'my own way' cannot be separated from the rest of reality. Resignation is the attitude of the ego, the separate self, thwarted by reality – and resentfulness. Surrender lets go of such wilfulness, and the idea that the future must conform to my wishes. All shall be well.

So I paste another letter on my wall with surrender, not resignation. I kiss the scribbled rejection, dance with a sense of failure, and bless the one who tells me I am not what they are looking for. (2004: 18)

And how might Saul's or Samuel's lives have developed differently if they had managed to respond in such a spirit?

8

'What if?'

Jonathan and what might have been

———•◆•———

By insisting on floating the question ... by leaving open another way of understanding what is going on ...
                                        Walter Brueggemann

Jonathan is one of the most influential characters in this story, but as he is best known for his special friendship with David, his wider contribution is usually missed.

Jonathan first appears as a military commander in Saul's army, attacking a Philistine garrison in what appears to be a successful attempt to trigger a revolt against Israel's deadliest enemy (1 Sam. 13.3). The people muster, and the scene is set for Saul to fulfil his destiny and drive the Philistines back onto the coastal plains. But he fails to grasp this opportunity – made possible, like previous opportunities, through the initiative of others – and to see things through. Samuel declares that Saul's kingdom is doomed and that Yahweh is going to replace him with 'a man after his own heart' (1 Sam. 13.14). Chapters 13 and 15 offer a brief illustrated summary of Saul's rise and fall as king. He is condemned for not doing what he is commanded to do, and in order to emphasize how essential his obedience is, the narrative stresses the hold the Philistines have over Israel. The Philistines control the blacksmith industry, so the Israelites are unable to make their own weapons. Yahweh is their only hope. Absolute trusting obedience is essential.

The account resumes in chapter 15, where once again Saul is sent into battle and only partially obeys orders. His disobedience leaves Yahweh unable to fulfil his purposes, and Yahweh now speaks directly, confirming his decision to replace Saul as king. Samuel and Saul have a further confrontation and their relationship breaks down beyond repair. Though Saul tries to repent, it is all too late.

But we race ahead. While the story unfolds in broadly chronological sequence, an 'episode' is suddenly inserted into the midst of it, without explanation. Chapter 14 is an instance of 'episodic narration', one of the storyteller's favourite devices.

The episode is about Jonathan, and interrupts a passage cataloguing Saul's failings and rejection as king. Though we have already met Jonathan as a military commander, only now do we discover that he is in fact Saul's son. This information is repeated four times (from the end of chapter 13). We learn that Jonathan is tactically astute, fearless, successful, and that he inspires great loyalty among his troops who are willing to follow his most risky initiatives. Jonathan is his own man – bold, energetic, able to act independently (and more wisely) than Saul, and Yahweh is with him. Isn't this, in fact, what a real king is supposed to be like? Jonathan's father, in the meantime, is rashly decreeing that his troops must not eat or drink on pain of death, until they have completed their victory. The result is a famished and dehydrated army. Initially unaware of the command, Jonathan eats and on being told of Saul's decree, is openly critical of it. 'My father has stirred up trouble for the land' (1 Sam. 14.29, Alter).

The episode now reaches its climax. Saul seeks divine guidance before going into battle, but Yahweh is silent. This is assumed to be due to a sin committed by someone in his army. Saul makes another rash declaration – 'even if [the guilty one] is my son Jonathan, he shall surely die!' (1 Sam. 14.39). The audience can hardly fail to see the irony of this. Then, when the soldiers have all been cleared of blame by means of throwing a dice and only Saul and Jonathan are left, Saul says, 'Cast between me and Jonathan my son' (14.42, Alter). And this is exactly what the listener is being invited to do.

What if Jonathan had become king?

One of the sadder ironies of this period of history is that the 'official' failure is a king who has fathered a son who by any measure is an outstanding heir to the throne. All the other leaders in this narrative – Eli, Samuel and David – are undermined by sons who are corrupt, ungodly and rebellious. But when leadership fails it is not just those responsible who suffer the consequences. For all his gifts and qualities, the direction of Jonathan's life and career is directly determined by the demise of his father's. There is no discrimination between good and bad.

Is the storyteller inviting us to conclude that an opportunity has been lost? That would be a surprise, as speculating on what might have been is not usually thought to be healthy or helpful. It might also seem faithless if we want to believe that God has been involved. But the storyteller is wiser here than he may appear.

'What if' and 'if only' questions occupy a powerful place in our personal and community imagination. 'What if' questions are a consequence of living in a world of complex choices and uncertain outcomes. Every act of choosing is an act of excluding even more. Our lives are full of unexplored possibilities, of turnings *not* taken. 'I live with quantities of hindsight,' says a recently retired friend after a long and varied career. Nor had any choice been a simple 'right' or 'wrong' for him, which suggests that our personal and community history-telling is always a work of reconciliation at some level.

We ask 'What if?' in the rawness of disappointment. In this world the wrong people are sometimes chosen or good appointments go unexpectedly wrong. Perhaps discernment has been lacking or critical factors were not clear. Unforeseen events may have changed a task and therefore the gifts that were needed. Choosing is always a fallible process, and in this story we notice that appointments go wrong *even for God*. Yahweh, too, knows the feeling that 'this was meant to turn out so differently'.

'What if' questions are part of the way we try to work out how we have arrived at where we are. Only a community or organization that can learn from, and reflect intelligently on, its past history of choices and outcomes will be able to take responsibility for the challenges of the present, and plan wisely for its future. That is why a core command in the Bible is to 'remember'.

Negatively, our 'what if' questions can lie simmering just below the surface, reflecting a brooding resentment of the present. This is not what we asked for. We were hoping for something very different. But it is debilitating for a community to refuse to live and work with what is given (after all, the world they would prefer exists only in their imagination!), and sad that the leadership on offer in such circumstances often seems to disappoint. The leader may become a scapegoat without ever quite knowing why – and not always because they have got anything *wrong*. Good leadership invites people and communities to places where they may choose to grow, take responsibility, and become leader-full. But if they decide *not* to develop, they will need someone to blame. 'No good deed goes unpunished,' as the saying goes.

I have sat on interview panels that have made appointments to a variety of leadership posts in recent years. Often, after the last candidate has come through, I've noticed a lingering sense of disappointment in the air that the someone we hoped for and *needed* has not turned up (regardless, I stress, of the competence of candidates for the task). Institutions under enormous pressure, working anxiously but bravely with dwindling resources, can experience great longings, and 'what if' dreams can be very hard to let go of. Wouldn't it be wonderful if our idealized king/leader/messiah/parent figure walked through the door, took over the Task/the Problem/the Diocese/the World and made it 'all right'? There is a huge market of heroic leadership books catering for these messianic hopes.

'What if' thinking in business is an important and responsible aspect of risk assessment. By this means we calculate what resources to hold in reserve against the demands of unforeseen events, and so ensure long-term security.

Part of the way the Church of England has done 'what if' planning at a senior personnel level is by filing the names and details of over 400 clergy reckoned by their diocesan bishops to have potential for senior leadership in the Church. This has traditionally been called the 'Preferment List' – a name that has unfortunate resonances with the closed world of gentlemen's clubs and of patronage by the privileged. Only in recent years has anyone known or even been consulted about being entered on the list at all!

I have found myself listening to and supporting a number of Church of England clergy involved. Of course, I am meant to know nothing. The proceedings are intended to be strictly secret – that much, at least, they have in common with senior appointments in 1 and 2 Samuel.

In practice, the experience is very uneven. Even the most personally secure of candidates going onto 'The List' feel as if they have been called up and then left on stand-by. And although the process of support and consultation has been improved, the Institution often seems to display too little regard for the care and faith of those willing to offer themselves. For the majority, being entered on the List will be the furthest they get: this crowded pool of godly talent exists to supply suitable candidates for approximately 35 posts a year.

Here we see institutional thinking at work. We will never need all these people but why not keep reserves high? At its best, this 'what if' process is an attempt to plan well and make good use of gifts and resources. But at what point does it become an act of trustlessness and exploitation? To take a metaphor closer to the world of Saul, isn't this a form of conscription? And didn't Yahweh warn the people about exercising power outside the constraints of trusting faith? The Institution as leader has a tendency to 'take'.

We often fail to recognize that this is a theological issue. One of the recurrent themes of God's ways with his people in the Bible is that he chooses and works through the *least*. Hannah's song declared this. The selection of Israel as God's people reveals it too. *God's ways and purposes are made known through, not in spite of, the willed vulnerability of his people.* And it is not the job of any strategy or development programme to redress this. Going into battle with Yahweh in this world always means going in with *less* than you need.

'What if' questions can sometimes have a prophetic quality to them.

I was invited to attend a conference focusing on issues of disability, faith and theology. It drew 400 people (nothing on this scale had ever been attempted before), many with serious physical impairments. Some outstanding speakers, all with experience of impairment in their own lives, offered their vision of wholeness and Christian living. The worship and stories shared through the day were inspiring and deeply challenging. There was no room for triumphalism in such company, and that day has stayed with me as an 'episodic' narrative – a 'what if' moment inserted into the 'main' story of a world obsessed with youthfulness, physical beauty, vibrant health, independence and endless personal choice. The first Christians were taught two core principles about the new community of faith they were now a part of. 'From now on, therefore, we regard no one from a human point of view' (2 Cor. 5.16) and, using the human body as an example, 'the members of the body that *seem* to be weaker are indispensable, and those . . . that we think less honourable we clothe with greater honour' (1 Cor. 12.22–23, my italics). This is a charter for a quite different way of knowing and being community. Many of those attending that day had painful stories of churches in which the teaching and worship unthinkingly mirrored the discriminatory assumptions about 'normality', 'attractiveness' and 'usefulness' of the surrounding culture. The conference broke into 'normal' daily life and faith, and by refusing to treat disability, faith and theology as a fringe 'special needs' issue, provided a powerful 'what if' glimpse of another way of belonging, of being human, of hoping and of knowing God.

Where might a 'what if' conversation about the significance of Jonathan in this story take us? Without ever being idealized, Jonathan is presented as the most integrated, loyal, relationally aware and emotionally literate of all the male personalities in this history (there is more choice among the women). He is able to sustain relationships in the midst of destructive and dangerous conflict. He maintains a personal freedom and initiative in situations of high anxiety and confusion. He is the one who enables David to survive Saul's attempts to kill him and thus ensures Israel's greatest king actually reaches the throne in the first place.

We meet Jonathan first as an adventurous risk-taker. Faced with the same opportunities as his father, Jonathan is able and willing to be decisive. He makes things happen. Twice we read of him embarking on wild, swashbuckling raids on the Philistines. In this he is close to the character of David and you can imagine the two of them thriving on the cut and thrust of wilderness campaigns where the odds are stacked against them. He is also a man of faith – uncomplicated, direct and hopeful faith, in a world where trust in God is often surprisingly absent. He prays. And as he plans his second attack on the Philistines with his servant, he adds his hope of God's blessing. 'It may be that the LORD will act for us; for nothing can hinder the LORD from saving by many or by few' (1 Sam. 14.6). His soldiers follow him – one of the most basic tests of a leader. 'Do whatever your heart inclines,' says his servant, 'here I am with you, my heart as yours' (1 Sam. 14.7, Alter).

Jonathan does not confuse loyalty or obedience with subservience. He can act independently. He is not a 'yes man'. Unbound by loyalty to his father, he can actually try to influence him for the better. He is a person who can speak truth to power. For the novelist Graham Greene, the key mark of a mature believer was 'a certain capacity for disloyalty'. Mature believers will never be found 'just following orders' – and are therefore unlikely to commit atrocities. They will always be capable of asking important questions or confronting others when necessary. They will on occasion express godly obedience in *dis*obedience. Jonathan risked his life in the middle of the conflict between Saul and David. He endured the furious denunciations of his increasingly unstable father (1 Sam. 20.30) and in this way became the means by which David was kept alive and able to take the throne.

Jonathan is a person who can love, commit and give himself freely. Large-hearted, impulsive and generous, he inspires these same qualities in those around him. His attraction to David is immediate, deep and passionate. 'Jonathan's very self became bound up with David's, and Jonathan loved him as himself.' (This is stated twice: 1 Sam. 18.1–2, Alter.) His commitment, once made, is unwavering. Sometimes we make up our minds very quickly about someone, usually when we recognize something of ourselves in the other person to a significant degree. David and Jonathan have a great deal in common, and though David fails to reciprocate Jonathan's commitment to their relationship, Jonathan never withdraws his love. He is not the kind of person who waits to count the cost.

Jonathan is willing to be acted upon. He must respond to the powers that be and manage the consequences of the achievements or failings of others. He must find his own path and purpose through the complexity and dangers of the agendas of others. It will not be for him finally to lead in his turn. In this respect, he occupies a place perhaps more familiar to women in this patriarchal society. His role is to negotiate a way between the king, who is his father, and his dearest friend who will replace him as heir to the throne. He is, in short, a servant leader. I have friends who have made something of a godly career of this way of being. Wherever they have gone they have worked in a deputy role behind the official leader, and very often theirs is the leadership that has mattered most. Of course, this may not be acknowledged, and the cost of working loyally under (possibly failing) leadership can be considerable. If we take on that role, our own potential for further responsibility may not be explored or even recognized, and we may have to consciously sacrifice our ambitions. But every organization needs its Jonathans: someone who through everything retains a certain humanity and in doing so inspires those around them to reverence theirs in contexts capable of becoming horribly inhumane.

Jonathan can lay down leadership. The most significant moment in the story comes when Jonathan freely yields his leadership to David. 'Jonathan stripped himself of the robe that he was wearing and gave it to David, and his armour, and even his sword and his bow and his belt' (1 Sam 18.4). In that action he symbolically lets go of any claim to the throne, and in his capacity to surrender power becomes what Simon Walker calls an 'undefended leader' (2007).

We have no way of knowing if Jonathan felt called to kingship. We are not told what it meant to him to be heir to the throne and to realize that he would never be king, as a consequence of his father's rejection. We do know that he was willing to play his part in the unfolding story – even if that meant being prepared to lay down his own life.

There is something about this man that anticipates gospel living in the midst of worldly power. He points to qualities of faith and leadership revealed most fully in Christ. For though (to paraphrase Phil. 2.6) Jonathan was in the form of a king, he did not cling to kingship, but emptied himself and became a servant.

9

Nobody does it better
David, man and king

————◆•◆•◆————

All theology, properly so called, is written in blood.

Harry Williams

'Be wise as serpents and innocent as doves,' Jesus told his followers (Matt. 10.16). What exactly did he mean? In the traditional version of the Church of England ordination service there was a prayer that candidates would be filled 'with all innocency of virtue . . . in the midst of this naughty world'. But no one ever prayed that they would become snakes. Wasn't that part of the call too?

I sometimes quote those words of Jesus to groups of leaders and ask them to list what qualities they think he had in mind. When it comes to the character of snakes they have no trouble filling the page, usually amid a good deal of laughter and mischief-making. The dove page section is generally slower going. Qualities of goodness, purity, harmlessness are mentioned, but by comparison these feel bland, 'worthy' and certainly less fun. Just how can snakes and doves coexist in one personality?

Innocence is usually thought of as a kind of virginity, as something preserved only by the sustained avoidance of worldly experience. But Jesus' *command* to be innocent suggests something we must *learn* rather than something we are born with. Innocence comes through engagement, not withdrawal. Just as a snake lives close to the ground – cunning, watchful, no one's fool, piercingly observant of the world's capacity for light, shade, duplicity, deceit and manipulation – so innocence lies in seeing with just the same clarity, but without being formed by, or passing on, the world's power to corrupt. Perhaps another word for this kind of innocence is holiness.

King David, the flawed genius who dominates this whole ancient era, had no need to pray for snake-like qualities. He possessed them in abundance. His struggle, throughout his life and reign, was to learn innocence.

The storyteller introduces David into the narrative with great subtlety. Having rejected Saul, Yahweh sends Samuel to the family of Jesse in Bethlehem to anoint the man chosen to succeed Saul as king. Samuel is nervous of Saul hearing what he is up to, and needs tactical advice from Yahweh on how to go about things (1 Sam. 16.1–3). Jesse's first son, Eliab, is presented and, just as he did with Saul, Samuel immediately judges by appearances: 'Surely the LORD's anointed is now before the LORD' (1 Sam. 16.6). He hasn't learned. But this time Yahweh interrupts and tells Samuel not to judge by outward appearances because he (Yahweh) 'looks on the heart'. (Listeners may wonder why this wasn't made clearer the first time around.) Jesse's next six sons are all rejected too. The eighth and youngest isn't even in the room, but out tending the flocks. David is sent for and once again his good looks are immediately stressed – 'he was ruddy, and had beautiful eyes, and was handsome' (1 Sam. 16.12). But Yahweh speaks decisively: 'this is the one', and David is secretly anointed.

This is the first (and most significant) of three consecutive stories that introduce David. They sit side by side, without reference to each other, and are at times even contradictory. Western storytelling tends to harmonize different accounts, but in Bible storytelling they are sometimes deliberately placed next to each other in a kind of dialogue. It is not our job to smooth out the differences: they are intended to reveal the diverse layers of influence at work in events as they unfold.

The second story starts with the disturbing news that Saul is being regularly terrorized by an evil spirit from Yahweh (1 Sam. 16.14–23). (In this ancient world there was no understanding of mental illness or of a separate world of evil and demons: signs of both are ascribed to Yahweh.) Under the pressures of kingship, Saul's personality and mental health have deteriorated and he is suffering recurrent bouts of depression and paranoia. Once again, others take the initiative for him. A servant suggests music therapy and recommends a young musician he knows. And so it is that David is found at the centre of Saul's court and personal life (and yes, his good looks and attractiveness are stressed again). Of course, the suggestion of *David* for this job was purely coincidental – or was it?

The third story is the most famous. The Israelites are facing the Philistines in battle and are being challenged to single combat by a huge warrior called Goliath (1 Sam. 17). The troops are terrified. A reward is offered, including the king's daughter, for the man who kills Goliath, and at this point the youngest brother of some of the soldiers arrives with food supplies. It is David, once again introduced as if for the first time. He watches and then volunteers for the job. Rejecting Saul's armour and weapons, he goes out to fight as the shepherd boy he is, with only a stick and his sling. As the youngest and the least, with all the odds stacked against him, David embodies the vocation of Yahweh's people in the world – and overcomes.

Our first story focused on revealing Yahweh's (hidden) sovereign will in human history. The other two are very public and proceed by a mixture of human initiative, natural ability, cunning and persuasive speech. But it is these two stories that lead directly into David's ascent to the throne, rather than the theological account of his direct but mysterious choice by Yahweh. As so often in this history, theology is required to defer to power and politics.

Old Testament theologian Walter Brueggemann calls one of his studies on this narrative *Power, Providence and Personality*, thus providing a basis for reflecting on the dilemmas of life and faith that run through it. We can perceive that this three-way tension (between power, providence and personality) finds unique embodiment in the life of David, man and king.

David has personality to spare. He is quite irresistibly attractive. The very quality that at his anointing Yahweh warns is not relevant dominates all early responses to him. This handsome, heroic warrior, poet, musician and king is loved by all – Saul, Jonathan, Michal (his wife), the women of all the cities and towns, 'all Israel and Judah' (1 Sam. 18.3–20). And this should give us pause for thought. In contemporary celebrity culture, a particular 'Personality' can, for a while at least, seem to be everywhere – followed obsessively, with every word logged and every action recorded. If the Personality is a leader, this can seem wildly hopeful and exciting. But it is vital that we reflect on what is image and what is substance. Popular, devotional presentations of David tend to reflect the romantic idealizing of celebrity culture rather than the shrewd discernment of the storyteller. Trying to be like a dove and forgetting that snake-like qualities are necessary, too, always results in a kind of religious escapism.

It has been said that the last thing we realize about ourselves is the effect we have on others, and the problem with David's extraordinary power and attractiveness as a leader is that he seems to be quite unaware of it. He is someone who inspires love rather than gives it; he is the object of love while appearing to do nothing to encourage it. Note that he never actually declares his love to anyone in return.

'What have I done?' David asks in two places in the story at moments when the answer is perfectly plain to anyone watching (1 Sam. 17.29; 20.1). He is like a bewildered little boy here, baffled at the effects of his actions and unable to make the relational connections. 'The fact that he apparently lacked the capacity to commit himself in the way people commit themselves to him would be unsurprising if the whole business of the way he won people's love was a mystery to him' (Goldingay 2000: 139).

For those who know David through the sensitivity of his psalms, this kind of emotional compartmentalizing is hard to comprehend. But it would explain in part his struggle to relate effectively to his own children, which brings him close to losing the throne, and his difficulty in relating to women. Did he really not realize how destructively he treated his wife Michal? Or that Absalom's intention towards Tamar was evil when he gave the permission that led directly to her rape? (2 Sam. 13).

A leader may not display patterns of emotionally dysfunctional behaviour when first appointed, but the pressures of the role can be highly damaging. You only have to compare the photos of national leaders from early and late on in their tenure to see the kind of burden they are required to carry.

There is an isolation in leadership that easily corrodes our capacity for relational commitment and warmth. Leading in situations of sustained conflict or in an atmosphere of continual suspicion means that you often do not know where the next attack is going to come from or who you can trust. I recall a bishop commenting that the biggest single burden on starting his job was coping with the sheer volume of negative post he received.

People who end up in positions of high responsibility in any career may find themselves separated from precisely where they are most alive and energized – and where their gifts were first noticed. David clearly thrived in the outdoor world, in the camaraderie of the campaign, against the odds in the wilderness, in the tactical cut and thrust of battle. Life in the palace seemed to sap him of his initiative and discipline.

It is also true that leaders can give out so much that they have little energy left for faithful love. All relationships become work. Not everyone is able to sustain the warmth of friendships in which they can be truly themselves.

David's friendship with Jonathan was clearly the most significant relationship in his life. The two are famously described as making a covenant together and much has been made of this in literature about love and friendship. But the English translations tend to conceal an essential detail in the story. There were different forms of covenant in that ancient world and the Hebrew makes clear that in this covenant the initiative is with the first named person: Jonathan. David accepts the covenant but does not reciprocate (20.16). Only at one of their last meetings does he show a dawning realization that he can trust this friend, and in that moving scene both weep, but 'David wept the more' (1 Sam. 20.41). 'Jonathan took David as close to loving someone as David could go, and he did so by being like him and loving him. Perhaps David thereby almost became able to love himself and therefore love someone else' (Goldingay 2000: 136).

Power is certainly key to understanding David. He is a calculating man and a calculator values power over love. He does not make covenants; he negotiates contracts. He displays the qualities of a snake, being shrewd, inventive, manipulative and cunning. He feigns madness to escape capture and execution (1 Sam. 21.13–14). He pretends to defect to the service of the Philistines to keep his distance from Saul. But sometimes, surely, he takes things too far? During this time we learn that he was also systematically wiping out whole towns around the borders, deliberately leaving no one to tell the tale (1 Sam. 27). Today he could be tried for war crimes.

Another side of David is deeply principled. He refuses to drink the water that his soldiers have braved enormous danger to bring him (2 Sam. 23.16–17). He turns down clear opportunities to kill Saul out of respect for the Lord's anointed (1 Sam. 24, for example), even taking the chance to appeal to Saul's better judgement. He will become king but it must be in Yahweh's time; he will not force the issue for his own ends. He is a person of prayer and faith, whose deepest impulse is to the service of his God. And finally, he is a leader you can speak truth to. When Nathan the prophet confronts him over Bathsheba and the murder of her husband Uriah, he listens and repents deeply. He also pays heed to Abigail as she risks all to shrewdly steer him away from violent intent (1 Sam. 25.14ff.).

We have observed before how the first words a person speaks in these stories capture their core character. David's opening line, spoken as he observes Goliath, is, 'What will be done for the man who strikes down yonder Philistine?' (1 Sam. 17.26, Alter). Though he then adds a pious comment about the insult to God, his primary motivation is clear and he spends the next few verses checking details of the reward among the troops to make quite sure. 'What's in it for me?' is not the popular, devotional image of this handsome man after God's own heart. It is not a line found in any of his psalms.

In contrast to Saul, everything the early David says and does is politic, astute and calculating. No personal feelings or vulnerabilities are revealed, right up to the defining episode of his life (and of the monarchy and of Israel itself) – his rape/seduction of Bathsheba. Only after the death of their son does a more vulnerable man emerge (2 Sam. 12.23). The tension between power, love and accountability fluctuates unevenly throughout the rest of his days without ever quite finding resolution.

At one level a reluctance to commit may enable a leader to separate from their role and exercise the ruthlessness a task sometimes requires. But the temptation to simply exploit and manipulate will be very real. It was a wise old priest who counselled someone considering a call to ordained ministry with the words, 'If you are going to be ordained in the Church of England you need almost as high a doctrine of corruption as you do of glory.'

When the then British Prime Minister Tony Blair was asked in interview about his faith, his press officer famously interrupted with the statement: 'We don't do God.' Well, it is not always clear that David did either. But though he functions successfully as a hard, shrewd politician for periods of this history, politics alone is not enough. Theology alone is not enough either. We 'do God' in the midst of raw and complex human dilemmas. Without such engagement, faith tends towards a detached piety, a false innocence that feeds on idealized assumptions about God and projects unrealizable expectations onto our relationships and our world.

The final accounts leading up to the end of David's life actually spill over into the first chapters of the book of Kings. We met the young David through three stories and by this reading of events, his life closes with three more.

The first is a disturbing episode near the end of the Samuel narrative (2 Sam. 24). Yahweh, we learn, is angry. He 'incites' David to conduct a count of the population (a strange and unexplained word to use here). Yahweh uses the word for a general population count – a census. But by the time David passes on this command to his officers the word has changed to one used more commonly for military or tax purposes. At this point even Joab, his commander, challenges the wisdom of the order. The count is now far more than a bureaucratic task. We have to imagine 'swift runners, powerful horses, fearful royal agents invading old villages and settled relations . . . the long ruthless arm of the military intruding into tribal and village life' (Brueggemann 1990a: 352). Whatever Yahweh intended by his provocative command (which is never made clear) the outcome is to assess and mobilize military power. Brueggemann calls this state terrorism.

Perhaps David could only see and hear Yahweh in his own image and language, distorted by his own understanding of power and leadership. He could only interpret Yahweh by way of his own inclinations. And who doesn't do this?

Then, just as abruptly, David comes to a place of realizing the utter awfulness of what he has embarked upon. Though it began as Yahweh's angry command, the event is now treated as entirely David's initiative. He plunges deep into repentance. The whole episode has lasted 'nine months and twenty days' – the human gestation period (2 Sam. 24.8). The theme of motherhood and life-bearing, for good or ill, returns once again to this story. But here it is a man's work not a woman's. And it has brought only death, not life.

This grim story has an unexpected ending. David and Yahweh join in an act of mutual reconciliation. It is not only David who repents. So does Yahweh (2 Sam. 24.10–16). Both have ended up in this place of unspeakable cruelty. 'Yahweh repents of anger and remembers mercy. David repents of arrogance and remembers trusting, submitting faith' (Brueggemann 1990a: 354). A new relationship is now possible. If nothing else, this is a very daring piece of theological storytelling.

Two final accounts follow in the early pages of 1 Kings as this legendary monarch approaches his end.

David is now very frail. The one who all his life had basked in the unsolicited warmth and adulation of others is shivering in bed, under numerous blankets, quite unable to get warm. His servants search the country and bring him a beautiful young virgin to keep him warm. But to no avail. He is now impotent (1 Kings 1.1–4).

We finally listen to him briefing Solomon, his son and heir. Frail though he is, these are the words of a tough old mafia chief wanting to ensure that no old scores will be left unsettled after he has gone. The scene is chilling in the extreme (1 Kings 2.1–10). David, man and king, remains an enigma to the last.

But if we close where the storyteller of 1 and 2 Samuel leaves us, we find ourselves in a different place. Just as it began, the story ends with someone presenting themselves alone before Yahweh in prayer. Like Hannah, David is empty and powerless. He has only bare and desperate faith, and in Yahweh alone lies his hope. Exposed to the barrenness of his life and reign he casts himself upon Yahweh's gracious providence, as Hannah did before him.

The story of 1 and 2 Samuel began with a womb that Yahweh had closed and then graciously opened to new life and thus to a new history. At the far end of this narrative, as David repents and seeks healing for his cruelly misjudged ways, misappropriated power and still-born initiatives, he says, 'let us fall into the hand of the LORD, for his mercy is great' (2 Sam. 24.14). The word translated 'mercy' here means 'womb', and the only other time it is used in this entire story is when speaking of the womb of Hannah (Trible 1978: 39–59).

Like her, David casts himself upon the womb-like mother love of Yahweh who can yet bring new life to birth out of barrenness and death.

10

I AM

God, hidden and revealed

————•·•·•————

God did a strange thing in consenting to be known to Israel through the slippery and always ambiguous medium of stories. Ellen Davis

For many years Bristol Zoo kept white tigers. I have a childhood memory of a huge, otherworldly creature, pacing up and down inside a cage that seemed barely big enough to turn in. R. S. Thomas wrote a poem about one of these tigers. 'It was beautiful as God must be beautiful,' he begins. He goes on to wonder how life feels in such a restricting world, 'breathing as you can imagine that God breathes within the confines of our definition of him' (Thomas 1993: 358). Zoos no longer keep animals in such conditions. But whether God finds our attempts at theology any more spacious today is another matter. 'So much religion is an attempt to tame the wildness of God,' wrote Richard Holloway.

That God consents that this be so at all is, of course, extraordinary and a mark of quite unquantifiable graciousness. He allows himself to be spoken for and wills his purposes to be communicated in significant measure through the unreliable medium of human hearts, minds and words. He honours our freedom, and will not impose upon it. This is both liberating and frightening. God is asking us to be responsible. He is giving us a great deal of space.

In doing so, he must conceal himself. The very name of God in the 1 and 2 Samuel story reflects this. 'Yahweh' is Hebrew for

I AM, and was the name revealed to Moses at the burning bush, where the story of the liberation of God's people from slavery in Egypt began. I AM will therefore forever be associated with a God who hears, is present, loves justice, who is committed, who sets free, who saves. It is, of course, the name Jesus takes for himself in John's Gospel (John 10.7–11, for example).

But wherever this name occurs in English Bibles the word 'LORD' is substituted. There is a practical reason for this. When the Greek translation of the Hebrew Bible (known as the Septuagint) was produced, it followed the Hebrew belief that the name of God was so holy that it could not be uttered or written. The Hebrew word used instead of Yahweh was *Adonai* (meaning master). This was translated into Greek as *Kurios*, which translated into English as 'Lord'. So an ancient reverence of the name of God became, in another culture and time, a different name altogether. 'Lord' is more a title than a revelation. It comes laden with associations of worldly status, institutional privilege, territorial ownership, hierarchy and authority. It is formal, impersonal and exclusively male. I AM has none of that baggage. Is it really a name at all? It both reveals and conceals. It suggests presence and mystery. But it is overwhelmingly personal. I can address someone as Lord or Judge without any personal relationship. I AM has the immediacy of one who needs no definition or qualification. It is a name without adjectives.

A few years ago, while struggling through one of those arid periods of faith when God seemed absent and the language of prayer empty, a wise guide suggested that I pray to Yahweh, to I AM. I have done so ever since. The impact was liberating and bewildering in equal measure. The name contains no familiar associations. It has no comparison and thus bypasses all our practised ways of knowing and being known. I AM is not defined by any task, achievement or characteristic. To pray to I AM is to find yourself with one who is both utterly present but indescribably other at the same time.

God's hiddenness is a central but neglected feature of the Bible. 'Truly, you are a God who hides himself,' exclaims Isaiah (45.15). In fact the defining difference between the true God and false gods in the Bible lies precisely in this – the true God *cannot* be seen. He dwells in cloud and thick darkness (Exod. 20.21). That is why there are such strict prohibitions upon the making of images of God. The New Testament teaches that he dwells in 'unapproachable light' and his ways are inscrutable (1 Tim. 6.16; Rom. 11.33). Similarly the Spirit of God is everywhere, but is both unseen and unknown: it 'blows where it chooses' (John 3.8). Followers of Christ are those whose lives are 'hidden with Christ in God' (Col. 3.3).

In the story of 1 and 2 Samuel, Yahweh's influence is everywhere but his presence is more often implicit than explicit; he is more hidden than revealed. Whole events unfold and are played out to their conclusion, for good or ill, without his (visibly) direct involvement – even when it seems desperately needed. The story of David and Bathsheba is one example. It begins, 'In the season when kings go to war ... David was sitting in Jerusalem' (2 Sam. 11.1–2, Alter). People found sitting in these stories are usually guilty of not fulfilling their vocation. David has sent others to fight his battles, and in his idleness intrudes upon the privacy of a woman bathing. He is tempted and 'sends' for her. 'Send' occurs repeatedly through the story. Royal power, by divine delegation, is repeatedly misused, leading to adultery and murder. At the end of the detailed narrative we read, 'and she bore him a son, and the thing that David had done was evil in the eyes of the LORD' (2 Sam. 11.27, Alter). That something very wrong comes to birth here will be widely apparent: in fact, the consequence of David's adultery will undermine his entire reign. But only now do we discover that Yahweh had seen it all and was displeased. Why, we wonder, didn't he step in sooner? Then as now, Yahweh allows us the frightening freedom 'to do stupid things' (Goldingay 2000: 66).

Christian faith has traditionally taught the hidden ways of God in the world through the doctrine of providence. This is the belief that a greater, as yet unseen, story is running through the unfolding events of life. Though quite beyond us, this story never ceases to seek out our involvement and invites us to find our meaning within it. Walter Brueggemann talks of 'a hidden purposiveness that is relentless, yet beyond anyone's management or manipulation' (1990b: 16), while Frederick Buechner writes of a world continuously interacting with 'the upthrusts of an underlying providence . . . God under history, constantly sustaining it and occasionally breaking the surface with a visible act that emerges into plain sight, like the tip of a iceberg' (1991: xx). This providential care works even through our most misguided projects. So although Israel's request for a king amounts to a direct rejection of Yahweh's own kingship, we find it already anticipated: Yahweh allows it and uses it to further his ways. Providence is trusting that God works with infinite responsiveness through the unfolding of human history. So it is that 'all things work together for good for those who love God' (Rom. 8.28).

But trust in providence is not a guarantee of certain desired outcomes – even for God. We discover that our freedom costs God. It wounds him.

There is a shocking moment in the Samuel stories that reveals this very clearly. 'I regret that I made Saul king,' says Yahweh to Samuel (1 Sam. 15.11). This could mean 'I repent of' or 'I am sorry' – either way, Yahweh has changed his mind regarding Saul. How are we to understand this? Has Yahweh been caught out by events he initiated? Has he made a mistake? The only other time Yahweh is recorded as speaking like this is back in Genesis, just before the flood, where we read that 'Yahweh was sorry that he had made humankind on the earth, and it grieved him to his heart' (Gen. 6.6). Elsewhere, the Hebrew word expresses acute mental and physical pain. It describes the hard labour of Adam in the stony soil of a world outside of Eden, and also the pains of childbirth (Davis and Hays 2003: 290f.).

From its earliest history, the Christian Church has struggled with the idea that the eternal God might be influenced by anything as unstable as human emotion. God must surely be beyond our fluctuating moods and passions. He is All Powerful (Omnipotent), All Knowing (Omniscient) and therefore Impassable (Unchanging), so how could God be caught out or distressed by anything that happens?

Pressed to its logical conclusion, this analysis of God presents him as unfeeling, unresponsive, impersonal, remote and utterly self-contained. Do we really find such a God revealed in the Bible or uniquely in the life and teaching of Jesus Christ? It is hard to imagine this God becoming a human being, and revealing himself through suffering, death and resurrection. G. K. Chesterton was daring but surely correct when he wrote: 'Christianity is the only religion in the world that has felt that omnipotence made God incomplete' (1996: 168).

Over the centuries, an important word used in relation to God and his character has been *apatheia*. This term needs careful handling. It is easily misunderstood, as it translates as 'detachment' or even 'indifference' (it is the root of 'apathetic') and at times has been assumed to mean those things. But God's *apatheia* towards his world is plainly *not* a remote, unfeeling detachment. God is love. How else do we understand the divine anguish and grief behind these words in 1 Samuel 5, over an outcome longed and hoped for that does not come about?

This God who can know deep and even anguished emotion has not 'broken down' or 'lost it', as we might. A God who changes his mind is not necessarily unreliable: in fact he is very good news. Precisely because he has no *need* to love or act, he can freely choose to. It is too easily assumed that to be free means having no commitments. But we do not have to look far to see the damage that results from such a belief. The Bible reveals a very different understanding of what freedom means.

Yahweh is a God who freely chooses not to abandon his world even in the face of utter faithlessness and rebellion. His own free nature presses him to act. In fact, our hope that life might find a new beginning out of crisis and chaos actually depends on God *not* having a commitment – at least, not one based on divine insecurity or need – to his people or to his world. As we saw in Chapter 4, Yahweh is a God who loves freely and chooses to work through the chaos of his wayward people and so can bring quite new possibilities to life within it. It is this freely committed God that the storyteller of 1 and 2 Samuel finds always at work within the uneven history of his people.

Apatheia is not only a quality of God's character; it is integral to Christian living in the world. *Apatheia* is a disciplined capacity to separate out what is essential and what isn't. It is a form of loving self-emptying in order to be available and attentive to what matters most; a detachment that makes real engagement possible. The Ignatian tradition of prayer sometimes describes *apatheia* as an 'active indifference'.

But is this not a strange time to be talking about detachment and hiddenness? The Church and the world are under huge pressure, beset with crises, longing to see a God who is demonstrably present and active. In such circumstances – as we wait impatiently and anxiously, looking for dramatic vindications of our hopes and prayers, willing to settle for short-term solutions – we are likely to regard the theological subtlety of the doctrine of the hidden providence of God as something of a luxury.

In fact, it is precisely at such times that the qualities of *apatheia* are needed most. The very moment that Israel was beginning life under a monarchy, Samuel issued a challenge and a warning. 'Fear not . . . but serve the Lord with all your heart. And swerve not after mere emptiness that will not avail or rescue, for they are mere emptiness' (1 Sam. 12.21, Alter). The most obvious meaning of 'mere emptiness' (in Hebrew *tohu*) is the fatal but hopeless attraction to false gods and false securities.

But the word is also found in the Genesis creation story: 'form-less' (*tohu*) is the world as yet unformed and unsustained by God's creating word (Gen. 1.2). To trust in what is *tohu* is to descend into non-being, into the void of a world unspoken. The warning could not be more stark. We have already noted how idolatry is the pursuit of the visible – something we can grasp, touch, measure and quantify. To 'swerve after' what is *tohu* in the Bible is generally to be attracted to what is *seen*.

Our world needs to embrace the saving *hiddenness* of God – a hiddenness that prises our fingers off all those attempts to grasp or control our own destiny, and teaches us a true *apatheia*. It is not the job of any strategy or training programme to minimize the importance of learning this, but in the anxiety and urgency of our daily lives we will struggle mightily to do so.

> While we are anxiously or ambitiously attached to any-thing we will not be capable of love or of truly knowing God. God is not useful. God does not serve any purpose, since God is an end in himself. However laudable our striving may be, as soon as God is used to achieve one purpose or another, we reduce the divine to an instrument. Then God is no longer God.   (Suurmond 1994: 29)

Our declarations of faith and religious policy-making may sound very spiritual; our intentions may be godly and sincere. But do our expectations of 'growth', 'renewal' and 'blessing' actually owe more to notions of our spiritual consumer rights than to living, vulnerable faith? It is perilously easy to proceed as if God is bound to our agendas and needs. If we just get the approach right, the budget and skills in place, display biblical soundness, *real* openness to the Spirit, and so on – then God must surely act, as if he is tied to all this and permanently on call. 'We are so preoccupied with God's relatedness, God being for us, that we do not attend enough to God's hiddenness. We do not know how to attend to God's own "Godness"' (Brueggemann 1986: 71).

There is a particular irony in the attempt of the Israelites to carry the Ark into battle as a visible sign of Yahweh's presence. It arrived with its full title: 'the ark of the covenant of the LORD of hosts, who is enthroned on the cherubim' (1 Sam. 4.4). But the Ark was always more a sign of absence than presence; the 'mercy seat' for Yahweh on the lid, formed by the outstretched wings of the two cherubim, was vacant. St John of the Cross saw in the emptiness of the Ark a reminder of the emptiness, the radical *apatheia* that is needed if we are to truly meet God (Kavanagh and Rodriguez 1979: 84).

Teachings on Christian spiritual life and maturing have always kept a special place for the experience of darkness and *not* knowing. Far from being a sign of the failure of faith or prayer, what is traditionally called the 'apophatic' way (meaning 'against image'), may be the one that forms us most deeply into the likeness of Christ. There will always be a creative tension between the apophatic and the perhaps more familiar 'kataphatic' way (meaning 'according to image'). For while we are right and faithful to seek to declare and make known the life of Christ in the world (kataphatic faith), we will also discover that the closer we truly come to God, the more inadequate our finite minds, imagination and words will prove for the task of comprehending him. Our growing towards God – who is gloriously greater than we can ever imagine – must always involve journeying into darkness and mystery (apophatic faith). In this sense, the apophatic way leads not to emptiness but to a truer fullness.

The apophatic tradition nurtures humility in us. It reminds us that all our ways of knowing, thinking and speaking about ourselves and God need cleansing, redeeming and utterly transforming. When we are under pressure for visible results, the apophatic way guards us from speaking carelessly or presumptuously about God. Even in our boldest missionary engagements, his mystery and unutterable glory will challenge us to display a reticence, a holy hesitancy.

For some years my work was to direct programmes for the training and support of people in ministry and leadership. There was much about this that was very fulfilling but I found that I could only sustain the intensity of the task by balancing it with a quite severe discipline of solitude and silence. Working in the fierce light of the Church's life required the discipline of attending to the dark. As often as I could, I would escape to meet with a wise hermit in a remote monastery on the Welsh borders. My times at the monastery were always harsh: praying there seemed as flinty hard as the hills, and there was a great deal of silence and often tears. But I never lost the sense that the tension I experienced was life-giving and life-sustaining, and that without it my vocation would actually be imperilled.

Of course, no two paths are alike. But as I continue to work alongside leaders in consultancy, mentoring and spiritual direction, I believe more than ever in the necessity for a robust apophatic theology to undergird the life and faithfulness of the Church.

The pressure to know, to be in control, to have the answers, is in the end unbearable. But in our tongue-tied struggles, on the outer margins of speech, sight and knowledge, as we resist as best we can the perverse appeals of 'mere emptiness' (*tohu*), we are found and held in the *un*knowability of One who is always in the midst of us. In the ancient world and in the present moment, this is the saving contradiction that is Yahweh.

11

Waiting among the dead

Vigil, protest and subversion

---·•◆•·---

*If in the beginning you weep, then subsequently you learn
to wait.*   Belden Lane

Every Saturday, women gather in Laleh Park, Tehran. At
first there were just a few; now the 'Mourning Mothers'
can number several hundred. They meet in silence, carrying
the photos of sons and husbands who, since the widespread
protests that followed the national elections of 2009, have
been imprisoned or killed by the Iranian security police.
Some of the Mourning Mothers have themselves been imprisoned, while the iconic image for the movement world-
wide is the face of the dying Neda Agha-Soltan, who was
shot by a police marksman during a peace demonstration.
The women pledge to go on meeting at 7 p.m. by the pond
close to where Neda died until there is an end to violence
on the streets and freedom for all arrested for participating in
peaceful protests. For their courage they endure severe beatings
by the police.

   Back in Israel's history, a woman called Rizpah was involved
in something very similar. For the most part, academic studies
on the Samuel narrative have ignored her, being more interested in the 'bigger' themes of political intrigue, the interplay
of powerful personalities and the succession to the throne. Who
is this woman to compete with all that? She is only a concubine
of the dead King Saul.

It is in this connection that we first hear of her existence. During a time of infighting and manoeuvring within the house of the late King Saul, Abner, then the most powerful of the players, was accused of having had sex with Rizpah and so of laying claim to Saul's power (2 Sam. 3.7). Rizpah's thoughts and feelings are, of course, not recorded. Like so many women in history she is voiceless, powerless and useful only as a means to an end – 'more possession than person' (Walker 2010).

She reappears some time later, however, still silent, still living out a life defined by the will and priorities of others. But now Rizpah takes an initiative. As a result, she moves to the centre of a story that begins with the nation in crisis.

'There was a famine in the days of David for three years, year after year' (2 Sam. 21.1). This would have been a catastrophe for such a small country, and though we do not know where this episode fits chronologically, the point is that it is clearly linked to David's reign. Why should this happen under a godly king? There must be a reason. Something must be wrong. Someone must be to blame. David seeks Yahweh's guidance and there emerges a story of unavenged blood-guilt: Saul had apparently violated a national vow by killing some Gibeonites. No historical evidence for this event is offered, and we only have David's word that it is the cause of the famine. An almost civil service neutrality is in evidence in the way the problem is defined, the cause identified and a strategy implemented that will 'solve' it. David meets with the Gibeonites, and in a parody of a negotiation process invites them to name their terms. What they want is entirely predictable and David agrees to hand over Saul's sons. The Gibeonites can now take complete revenge on their bitter enemies while David, we have to note, has conveniently disposed of the awkward threat of Saul's descendants. Once again in this narrative, a problem worthy of theological consideration is actually addressed through political expediency.

Saul's seven male descendants are publicly executed in his home town, and in a further act of desecration their bodies are left in the open air for the carrion to eat. There was no greater shame than this in the ancient world. But now Rizpah, mother of two of the dead, appears, and in silence she constructs a makeshift shelter over the bodies and keeps vigil in their honour – night and day, in the heat and cold, through the long summer weeks.

This is a very public wake and an act of extraordinary courage. Try to imagine it. She 'places herself, for a long period, in pure hell' (J. P. Fokkleman, in Walker 2010: 18).

Such stories are all too familiar around the world today. Women still wait – in food queues, for water supplies, outside police stations, at military checkpoints, by the bedside of children dying for lack of medication, in makeshift graveyards. They would identify with Rizpah all too well. They would know what holds her there.

In Argentina, women – the 'Madres de La Plaza de Mayo' – have kept a vigil outside the presidential palace for over 30 years. During a notorious era in their country's history known as the Dirty War (1976–83), the military junta ruled by terror. At least 60,000 civilians are known to have lost their lives. An estimated 500 children of murdered mothers were given to military families for illegal adoption. Early in the movement, three founder members of the group were themselves murdered.

A similar story unfolded in Chile where, in a haunting expression of love and protest, women would meet outside the notorious police headquarters where their men had been tortured and murdered by the military dictatorship, and sway and move as if in the arms of their loved ones. The rock musician Sting set this scene to music in a song he called 'They Dance Alone' (*Cueca Solo*, 1987).

There is a kind of waiting in this world that is a consequence and a critique of power. It is the experience of the dependent, the poor, the voiceless – those whose needs and options are constrained by the choices and priorities of others.

In fact, waiting exercises a defining influence upon all of us. How we choose what matters to us, who we ignore and who we assume to be important, whether we give or grasp, are all shaped, for good or ill, by our attitude to the practice of waiting. That we live in a society with little or no positive place for waiting is evident, for example, in the continually stated priority in political manifestos to reduce waiting. We are a chronically impatient culture and our expectations of those who lead us reflect this. We place huge demands on our leaders and allow them very little time to come up with the goods.

It should hardly surprise us, then, if patterns of public leadership adapt in response. I recall a conversation with the CEO of a local government authority, who noted that the average length of tenure for people in jobs like hers was just two years. The same could be said for key national government posts. And not only is the turnover of leaders high: an adversarial political system means that people are defined by how *different* they are from whoever has gone before. Each new person has their own 'big idea', which they may impose without regard to actual need or to what has gone before (after all, they may well not be in post long enough to manage the consequences!). A notorious 'bonus culture' compounds this championing of discontinuity by actually rewarding inattention to longer-term planning.

As a result, the management of whole areas of society is effectively being tackled with only a short-term agenda in mind. Local church leaders, who are among those who share a longer-term vision of community development, often find that they are continually starting again when it comes to relating to local government officers.

As I write, President Obama, just three years into a term of office that began with such fresh optimism, is being heavily criticized for not delivering changes that clearly require more time. In the UK, a reviewer of Tony Blair's autobiography, *A Journey* (2010), offers a novel perspective. Reflecting, not uncritically, on the exceptional leadership qualities of the former Prime Minister, he suggests that his experience makes him ready to *start* the task of leadership – at the very moment he is setting it down.

Leaders and communities whose lives are shaped around *not* waiting need to ask themselves what it is they are trying to avoid. A man came to see me to reflect on his vocational and spiritual development. He was a gifted leader and the conversation was lively and stimulating. But afterwards I found myself asking if he, himself, had ever actually arrived in the first place. When he paused, it was only until another idea caught his imagination and then he was off again. Heady stuff, and the thoughts were exciting, but what did it all mean if the real person was effectively absent? My attempts to create a waiting space largely failed. Ideas were being used to cloak an emptiness he clearly lived in terror of facing.

I recalled the terse wisdom of the Sufi poet, Rumi:

> . . . just be quiet and sit down.
> The reason is: you are drunk,
> And this is the edge of the roof.   (Bly 1999: 168)

I am suspicious of leadership programmes that give no place to the discipline of waiting. Without this, 'leadership' will remain part of the problem – something driven by the latest ideas and prey to all the familiar illusions about its own power and importance. Even the most godly leaders can show almost brutal disregard for those most impacted by the consequences of their decisions. A friend with considerable experience of working with those in senior church leadership stresses the priority that must be given to waiting in these pressured times:

> It is easy to panic. The strain on bewildered clergy and bishops to get some results, to turn some tide, is enormous. Even when we have read up on the analysts and socialists and organisational theorists, is there still something we

don't know we don't know? Something that would allow us to wait in the ruins of the Church with patience, equanimity, faith and hope?

(Tim Marks, quoted in Runcorn 2008: 18)

A resistance to waiting is nothing less than an inability to be present – to ourselves, to our world and to God. When we display this attitude, 'our lives take the form of an absence' (Whyte 2001: 60). Life unnurtured by the discipline of waiting becomes dehumanized, whereas there is something in the stature of waiting that restores our basic humanity. Leadership can be redeemed by the capacity to wait, as our sensitivity to consequence is reawakened, and we begin again to pay attention, to listen, to notice.

Waiting, rather than activity, may be the most essential quality of Christian presence in a world like ours. For Alan Amos, whose experience has been shaped by living through some of the most violent periods of the Middle East's recent history, silent waiting became a valued way of prayer.

> The difficulty is that words have lost their meaning. For instance, if you mention hope you might as well be talking about despair for all the effect it has. Therefore I would talk mostly of waiting upon God and quietly searching for his presence. Real prayer is offering what you can see and grasp of what is happening, however painful it is, and waiting on God with it, almost as if you have it in your hands.   (Alan Amos, in Runcorn 1990: 126)

When we speak of what it is to be made in the image of God we tend to stress active, positive qualities of co-creating. But Rizpah reminds us that we are also called to a kind of co-waiting, co-enduring. It is not easy to find a name for this, but it has something to do with pain-bearing and cross-bearing (Vanstone 1982: 101ff.). It involves waiting, beyond words and strategies.

Back on the bare hill top outside Gibeah, far from policy-makers, planners or pray-ers, Rizpah sits silently beside the rotting corpses of her sons and their half-brothers. She drives away the vultures and the wild dogs. She watches and she waits, and at the end of that long, dry summer the rains return at last. The famine is over – but not the story.

When King David finally hears what Rizpah has done, he gathers up not only the bodies of the seven sons of Saul but also those of Saul and Jonathan, and gives them all a proper burial. Whatever reason was claimed at the start of the story, Yahweh acts only after David has been shamed into honouring the remains of Saul, Jonathan and the male line by Rizpah's vigil. Only then, we hear, did God 'grant the plea for the land' (2 Sam. 21.14, Alter).

When the world of biblical studies ignores Rizpah or treats her as a mere detail in a narrative with more important elements, doesn't this reveal the same unthinking prejudice that the storyteller here exposes? His style is to hold up a mirror to his listeners, rather than to confront them. It's up to us to reflect whether the assumptions we are making about who is powerful and significant are distorting our attention.

The story of 1 and 2 Samuel begins and ends with songs that celebrate a different kind of world. In Yahweh's kingdom, those who presume to have power are brought down and the voiceless, the poor and marginalized are raised up to a special place. Hannah is the embodiment of this principle, which will later be celebrated in the song of Mary. Jesus' radical ministry is undergirded by it too, leading him to seek out and bless the most inappropriate people – to scandalous effect.

In 1 and 2 Samuel, women are found at many of the pivotal moments in the drama: Hannah, Michal, Tamar, Abigail, Abishag, Rizpah, the woman of Abel Beth Maccah and even the witch of Endor – all shape the direction and theology of the story. And by their words, their silence, their initiatives or merely their presence, they often provoke a subversive critique of the powers that use and claim to speak for them.

We might expect a Church founded on such songs and stories to readily reflect their teaching. But it has not been so. When I taught a course on Church of England history, I found it quite painful to lecture on the topic of men and women in ministry over the last hundred years. There was no disguising the persistent institutional bias in favour of men and the sustained exclusion or exploitation of women. At one point, I came across a personal reflection by a respected theologian, then teaching in a ministry training college, which I keep with me still. It describes the experience of trying to participate in a historic institution whose patterns of life and thought have excluded the contributions of women for centuries.

A feeling somehow grew that, in the texts of theology, my women students and I did not exist. Something important about us and our lives had not gone into forming this rich doctrinal, liturgical and pastoral mixture. Somehow women's voices had not been heard, and we were all the losers for it. I remember thinking on one particularly grim day, 'It doesn't matter, because God loves women!' – and somehow, and to my surprise, this recognition made me weep with relief. Of course, I had never consciously doubted that God loved women. But somehow the barrage of ancient opinion, the structures into which one was perceived to fit oddly, the little niggling negativities which one felt in a place which fitted the male candidates like a glove, all conspired to make one feel that women were not really quite as good as men, that God didn't care about women *quite* as much as men, that women's sufferings (so many of them not even figuring on the ethics or pastoral courses) did not matter *quite* as much as those of men, that what happened to women in the home didn't matter

quite as much as what happened to men in the work-place.
In short, that somehow women didn't figure . . .

(Janet Soskice, in Walker 1993: 198)

Rizpah, alone, silent and empty-handed, presents a challenge
to theology, politics and leadership in this story. She reveals to
us the presence and will of Yahweh, who rather than sitting
with kings, enthroned on the high theology of Israel's institutional monarchy, is found waiting on a parched hill top outside
Gibeah, voiceless and sidelined. And Rizpah shares his vigil
with him. With Yahweh, she descends to the dead, where the
consequence of unredeemed power, theology and strategy lie
exposed for all to see.

Perhaps she ministers *to* Yahweh. She reminds us of the
women waiting and watching with Jesus at his cross. We might
also recall Jesus' insistence that how we treat the least, the most
needy and marginalized among us is how we treat him. 'As
you did it to one of the least of these who are members of my
family, you did it to me' (Matt. 25.40).

Rizpah's actions subvert the prevailing scripts. They rebuke
the powers that be. She calls David back to the core values of
respect, honour and service. And she reminds him, in so doing,
that these qualities reflect the likeness of Yahweh too.

12

Calling from the walls

From victim to witness

————•·•·•————

Those at the edge of any system and those excluded from
any system, ironically and invariably hold the secret for the
conversion and wholeness of that very group. They always
hold the feared, rejected, and denied parts of the group's soul.

Richard Rohr

Near the end of 1 and 2 Samuel there is a little-known short
story. It comes at a very bleak point in David's reign, which is
in danger of turning into an unredeemed saga of rebellion,
treachery and violence.

The land is soaked in blood. David has come close to
losing his throne to his son Absalom, and has even fled
Jerusalem. Absalom is now dead, but there is still unrest,
and much uncertainty about the loyalty of the northern
tribes. (At this time, the nation was divided into two parts.
David came from a tribe in the southern kingdom of Judah,
while Saul's tribe was part of the northern kingdom of
Israel. The significance of tribal and regional identities in
the struggle for national unity will be apparent to anyone
following the conflict in Afghanistan today.) David has
returned to the capital, but even in his palace he is diminished.
His concubines have been raped by Absalom – a standard way
of usurping the power of a rival king – and their cloistered,
childless fate now mirrors that of Michal, his first wife, who
'had no child to the day of her death' (2 Sam. 6.23). David

experiences difficulties in life-bearing and relating to others, to the last.

Sitting in his palace, he faces a second rebellion, which he fears even more than the first. A man called Sheba is gathering an army and heading north to make a base in one of the walled towns there.

David has sacked Joab, his chief commander. We are not told why, but it may be pertinent to note that David has survived as a leader by *not* trusting those around him. At this point in the story he appears as a lonely, anxious figure, issuing commands but not really in charge. There are many in leadership who could painfully identify with him.

David gives his new commander, Amasa, three days to muster an army. When Amasa misses this deadline, David promotes Abishai, Joab's brother, and sends him directly after Sheba without waiting for reinforcements. However, Joab has no intention of being so quietly sidelined, and the soldiers who now set out are called 'Joab's men' (2 Sam. 20.7). When Joab meets Amasa on the way, he tricks him with a show of friendship, then slashes open his rival's stomach so that he is left to a bloody and very public death in the middle of the road.

The story now takes us to the far north of Israel's territory, close to what would be the border with Lebanon today, to the walled town of Abel Beth Maacah. It is here that the rebel Sheba has made his base.

Before long, Joab's troops arrive and the town is besieged. The usual policy would be to reduce it to rubble and butcher the entire population, and there is something utterly sinister about the way the soldiers begin to go about this process. Faceless and silent, day after day, they 'batter' the walls (the word here can also mean 'savage', see 2 Sam. 20.15) in a terrifying manner. No warnings are issued and all escape routes sealed. There are many towns and villages in war-torn parts of the world today for whom the dilemma of which side to support in a conflict would be a matter of life and death. This town is not even offered a choice.

Suddenly a woman from the city appears on the wall. 'Listen! Listen!' she commands (2 Sam. 20.16). We know that her first words will define her character and vocation, and this woman is obviously someone who listens and who can teach others to do so. If the present story is to have a different outcome, the soldiers must stop what they are doing and pay attention to her. We can imagine the hammering ceasing at this point, and an unexpected silence falling over the walls.

The woman asks to speak to Joab and tells him to 'listen' too. Though shrewdly deferring to him as his 'servant' (not the first woman to suss that men listen better if allowed the illusion that they are still in charge!), she is clearly running the negotiations. Joab affirms, 'I am listening'.

The woman has taken a big risk with this initiative. She could have been killed for her effrontery. But her presence is calm, competent and non-anxious. As a result, it is possible for those involved in a volatile situation, on the brink of descending into pitiless violence, to view it from a quite different perspective.

The woman first introduces Joab to the town he is about to destroy. 'We have a long established reputation in the region for wisdom and mediation skills,' she tells him. 'Ask anyone around here.' The woman then declares her loyalty to the king and her commitment to peace, before confronting Joab: 'You seek to put to death a mother city in Israel. Why should you engulf the LORD's heritage?' (2 Sam. 20.19, Alter).

Once more, the theme of motherhood comes to the fore as an expression of Israel's vocation. This loyal town, whose inhabitants have the kind of skills the current situation badly needs, is placed centrally within the life and purposes of God. Unconsulted throughout this whole male-led campaign, Yahweh is finally named by an unnamed woman, obliged to risk death on her city walls.

Of course, Joab denies any intention to destroy the town: all he wants is the rebel Sheba. Having negotiated with Joab, the woman now goes 'in her wisdom' (2 Sam. 20.22, Alter) to guide her townsfolk through their response. Peace-makers they may be, but the townspeople prove themselves perfectly capable of making hard choices when the situation requires it. The head of Sheba comes flying over the wall and lands with a thud at Joab's feet. The northern rebellion is over.

A story that began with the blowing of Sheba's ram horn rallying 'everyone to their tents' now ends with the sound of Joab's trumpet. And his troops disperse, 'every man to his tent' (2 Sam. 20.22, Alter).

Notice what happens next. Joab returns from the peace-making city of Abel Beth Maacah to Jerusalem, which means 'City of Peace', but his only interest is in consolidating the political and military power of the state. He is named as commander in chief of all the army (2 Sam. 20.23). You wonder if he has really learned anything at all from recent events. Did he consider, for example, bringing the wise woman to the court as an adviser? And if not, why not? Worse is to come. In a chilling development, a new post appears in the list of government officials: a minister for 'forced labour' (2 Sam. 20.24). The Israelites, former slaves whose liberation from Egypt by Yahweh is legendary in their world, are now slave-owners. The very thing that Samuel warned the people would happen if they had a king is fulfilled.

There is, I believe, a direct relationship between the failure to listen and the experience of work as a form of forced labour. I've found this to be true for me personally, and have observed it among those I meet with for consultancy or spiritual direction. Without a disciplined, listening heart, a leader or minister (or anyone for that matter) will be driven by the tasks they face. If we don't have the reflective space we need to re-imagine the world, our only option will be to work *harder*.

Edwin Friedman insists that this is the biggest single problem facing our Western society in terms of its patterns of leadership. He discerns a culture closed in on itself and using endless varieties of programmes and strategies as 'systems of salvation', driven by messianic hopes for deliverance (2007: 5). Because so much is at stake and outcomes are so uncertain, these systems are held in place by very high levels of anxiety.

Anxiety is a powerful inhibitor in leaders and communities. Above all, it results in an inability to be present. When we're uptight we can't breathe (the Latin root of the word anxiety, *angere*, also means 'to choke'); we feel that life is closing in, leaving us fewer and fewer choices. In the grip of anxiety, our capacity to listen, love or respond imaginatively will be much reduced. An anxious organization or community will tend to react to issues that arise as 'problems' and seek 'solutions'. As a result, it is likely to over-invest in strategies and programmes, to overvalue 'professionals' and *certain kinds* of leadership (charismatic/messianic/'expert'/guru), and to over-rely on extraversion and activity. When we are anxious we fear chaos, and so strive for control and conformity. Our inclination is to exclude rather than embrace. And so our systems of 'salvation' become a form of forced labour.

When anxiety drives our responses to life we lead poorly, because our preoccupation is simply to survive. We will blame rather than assume responsibility. We will play the victim in order to avoid taking a stand or making critical decisions – and in so doing, actually victimize others (Jinkins 2003: 43). The primary but most demanding quality of a leader is to be *a non-anxious presence*. Knowing this, a wise work consultant once bluntly confronted a senior leadership team with the real task facing them: 'You will not get anywhere until you can admit what you are afraid of.'

Anxious, system-driven communities and their leaders suffer from 'gridlocked imagination' (Friedman 2007: 29). They display a fundamental inability to break out of the prevailing ideologies, inherited scripts and old ways of seeing. *They will be unable to recognize truly new possibilities for what they are.*

The story is told of a man who regularly passed four dogs and their owner when walking in the fields near his home. The dogs were all of the same breed, but while three of them bounded far and wide with uninhibited excitement and abandon, the fourth would always stay close to its owner and run round and round in very small circles. One day the man asked the owner why the fourth dog behaved in this way, and learned that it had spent most of its early life locked up in a cage, where running in tight circles was its only way of exercising. Although the cage was long gone, the dog was still living as though confined (Laird 2006: 19).

Sometimes we are unable to see beyond ourselves. We adopt a closed system of 'salvation', in which the system itself determines our choices, the outcomes and the way we explain those outcomes to ourselves and others. But it may be that the question we find ourselves endlessly trying to answer is one that actually needs reframing.

Israeli writer and political critic David Grossman offers insight into this concept as he comments on the difficulty his people have in moving towards peace initiatives.

> People who are born to war, programmed by war, their entire vocabulary is taken from war. It's tragic and we might not have the power to redeem ourselves from it. This is why we desperately need help from the outside. Time and again we choose warriors to lead us, but maybe by choosing warriors we doom ourselves always to be in wars. (*Observer* 2010)

The woman on the wall, who interrupts a story driven by a 'system of salvation', is just such a redeeming voice 'from outside'. Abel Beth Maacah offers a fleeting glimpse of another world, one in which things are done differently and have been for a long time. We noted that having talked to Joab the woman went to consult her people (2 Sam. 20.22). Where else in 1 and 2 Samuel has leadership taken this non-directive, non-coercive approach? This is the first instance we have seen of mediation in action in the community. In Abel Beth Maacah, peace-making is not regarded as problem-solving but as a way of life.

We have come to a second 'what if' moment (remember Jonathan in Chapter 8?). What if Joab and David had listened to the woman on the wall and allowed another way of thinking and acting to capture their imagination? Long years before, when the nation lived through a period in which they could not hear God, and his word was rare in the land, a new era of faith and leadership came through a young man who listened in the dark: 'Speak, LORD, for your servant is listening.' There is a fresh call to listen here, but sadly this wise woman and her town slip out of the story as quickly as they appeared in it, and we are left pondering a missed opportunity, as the state trusts in power and lurches towards oppression.

If we are unable to approach a challenging situation with 'outside' thinking, our boldest, most innovative initiatives will be constrained by our narrow assumptions about life, society, God, work. It is not that we require more information. After all, data doesn't energize, and measuring the task will just leave us struggling harder. What we really need is a way of going beyond our horizons, rather like the great maritime explorers of the late fifteenth century did at the beginning of the Renaissance in Europe. They simply sailed off the edge of existing maps and in so doing began to discover how much bigger the world actually was.

It is very hard for an anxious community or leader to be imaginative, to seek the space needed to reflect. For when we are stuck in a non-reflective world, where everything can be reduced to an object and defined by its usefulness and productivity, reality will appear to be devoid of mystery, and the imagination will seem just an inefficient distraction.

It is interesting to find a growing concern over feelings such as these within literature on work and leadership. David Whyte's use of poetry and art as a way of helping people to reflect on their work and identity is explicitly shaped by a compelling need to speak to the 'soul': 'There were hundreds of thousands of people out in the work world who frequently but secretly despaired of keeping their souls alive in the organisation for which they worked and desperately needed to reclaim a life they could call their own' (1994: xix).

My observation is that Whyte's diagnosis – 'The core of difficulty at the heart of modern work life is its abstraction from the ancient cycles of life that allow the silence and time in which true appreciation and experience can take place' (1994: 23) – is also true within the world of Church and faith.

Similar convictions are being expressed by writers on spirituality and prayer. Thomas Merton, Ronald Rolheiser, Margaret Silf, Kenneth Leech and other Christian guides (see Runcorn 2008: 20ff. and 2011: 182ff.) have long discerned the deep sickness of an age alienated from itself by its enslavement to technology, materialism and the pursuit of power. They believe that this can only be healed by the recovery of a contemplative, reflective spirituality. In all faith traditions, the contemplative disciplines of prayer and attentive listening have close links to the awakening of social conscience and the forming of resistance movements. They provide a way of deepening and maturing that helps lead people away from a religion of easy answers, from false certainties, from the idolatry of consumer spirituality, and from the lure of fundamentalism of all kinds. Without this necessary dimension, religion becomes too activist, task driven and pragmatic – even in its praying. It colludes with the powers of the age rather than offering a subversive and redeeming alternative.

The hunger for time to be still and to listen in popular approaches to spirituality and meditation today is a sign that we at least have some awareness of our need. But we should

beware if our approach seems more therapeutic than transformative. Contemplation cannot be defined as a withdrawal
from the pressures of a world we would rather not be a part
of and struggle to cope with, or as a technique to acquire
stillness. It is not limited to some particular temperaments
or about being quiet rather than active. What we meet in the
wisdom of the woman of Abel Beth Maacah and her community is the kind of tough listening that engages with and
confronts powers that appear overwhelmingly threatening,
and offers a quite different way of responding.

Such responses may find expression in very simple initiatives.
When I was vicar of a lively and resourceful church on the edge
of London, I became aware that we were tending to import the
driven approach to decision-making of the business culture
around us into our business and strategy meetings. Indeed,
people were often arriving for meetings straight from pressured
days in their workplace. So we agreed to a particular discipline
in our meetings: at a set time, no matter where the discussion
had got to, we stopped. I lit a candle and read one verse from
a psalm and we were silent for ten minutes. (I would time it.)
After that we simply resumed our business. Like the call of that
wise woman on the walls – 'Listen! Listen!' – we let the silence
disrupt our agenda. It was often very irritating for people. It
cut across all the familiar ways of behaving and messed up the
flow of thought. But we noticed a subtle change in the climate
of our meeting: a new humanity was in evidence, and I like to
think a spirit of wisdom now informed the decisions we took.

On the battered walls of a remote, vulnerable town, a woman
offers a way of transforming the world. In a situation of great
danger, she becomes a prophetic witness, while the state, for
all its powers, is revealed as a victim – trapped by its gridlocked
imagination, and driven by systems that can deliver only brutal
submission and conformity.

This nameless woman and her wisdom remind us of a pattern
we have noticed throughout the story of 1 and 2 Samuel. Time

and again, the significant turning points, the redeeming initiatives, the interpreting of meanings, and the breaking of deadlocks *have not been found at the centres of power*. The Institution is more often driven by anxieties about its preservation than by hopes for its transformation. Time and again, we have traced the true presence of Yahweh to the words, actions or faithful presence of people on the edge of the 'main' script. Hannah sang at the beginning of the story about the powerful being brought down and rendered voiceless, while the marginalized and those victimized were raised up. The vision and hard-won wisdom of this second group is what we need as we seek renewal. For only those who have stepped out in faith or been forced out by the systems 'are free enough from our obsession with security and control to dream a different world' (Mursell 2005: 76).

We are called to the honest, disciplined *attentiveness* that has shaped this extraordinary work of ancient storytelling. Our hope lies here – and nowhere else.

Sources and further reading

Alter, R. (1992) *The Art of Biblical Narrative* (New York: Basic Books).

Alter, R. (1999) *The David Story* (New York: Norton).

Alves, R. (1990) *The Poet, the Warrior, the Prophet* (London: SCM Press).

Bell, J. (1996) 'Unchaining the Male', *Third Way*, October.

Bly, R. (ed.) (1999) *The Soul is Here for Its Own Joy: Sacred Poems from Many Cultures* (New York: Ecco).

Brewin, K. (2004) *The Complex Christ: Signs of Emergence in the Urban Church* (London: SPCK).

Bridges, W. (2003) *Managing Transitions* (Cambridge: Da Capo Press).

Brueggemann, W. (1986) *Hopeful Imagination: Prophetic Voices in Exile* (London: SCM Press).

Brueggemann, W. (1990a) *First and Second Samuel* (Louisville, KY: Westminster John Knox).

Brueggemann, W. (1990b) *Power, Providence and Personality* (Louisville, KY: Westminster John Knox).

Brueggemann, W. (2002) *David's Truth in Israel's Imagination and Memory* (Minneapolis: Fortress).

Brueggemann, W. (2009) *Divine Presence Amid Violence* (Oregon: Cascade Books).

Buckmaster, S. (2004) 'Leadership and Gender: Let me count the ways', unpublished paper.

Buechner, F. (1991) *Now and Then* (San Francisco: HarperCollins).

Chesterton, G. K. (1996) *Orthodoxy* (New York: Bantam Doubleday Dell).

Davis, E. and Hays, R. B. (eds) (2003) *The Art of Reading Scripture* (Grand Rapids, MI: Eerdmans).

Dennis, T. (1994) *Sarah Laughed: Women's Voices in the Old Testament* (London: SPCK).

Donovan, V. (2001) *Christianity Rediscovered* (London: SCM Press).

Eagleton, T. (2009) *Reason, Faith and Revolution: Reflections on the God Debate* (New York: Yale University Press).

Firth, D. (2009) *1 and 2 Samuel* (Nottingham: Apollos).

Forster, E. M. (1991) *A Passage to India* (London: Everyman).

Friedman, E. (2007) *A Failure of Nerve: Leadership in a Quick Fix Society* (New York: Seabury).

Goldingay, J. (2000) *Men Behaving Badly* (Carlisle: Paternoster).

Hirst, J. (2006) *Struggling to be Holy* (London: Darton, Longman and Todd).

Jamieson, A. (2002) *A Churchless Faith: Faith Journeys Beyond the Churches* (London: SPCK).

Jinkins, M. (2003) *Transformational Ministry* (Edinburgh: St Andrew Press).

Journal of Extension (1995) 'A Framework for 21st Century Leadership': <www.joe.org/joe/1995december/a1.php>

Kavanagh, K. and Rodriguez, O. (1979) *The Collected Works of St John of the Cross* (Washington: Institute of Carmelite Studies).

Keller, C. (2003) *The Face of the Deep: A Theology of Becoming* (London: Routledge).

Kirsch, J. (1970) *The Harlot by the Side of the Road: Forbidden Tales of the Bible* (New York: Ballantine).

Kirsch, J. (2000) *King David: The Real Life of the Man who Ruled Israel* (New York: Ballantine).

Laird, M. S. (2006) *Into the Silent Land* (London: Darton, Longman and Todd).

Lane, B. (1998) *The Solace of Fierce Landscapes* (Oxford: Oxford University Press).

Lawrence, J. (2004) *Growing Leaders* (Oxford: BRF).

Le Guin, U. (1993) *The Earthsea Quartet* (London: Puffin).

Mourning Mothers of Iran: <www.facebook.com/pages/Mourning-Mothers-of-Iran/121906523071>

Mursell, G. (2005) *Praying in Exile* (London: Darton, Longman and Todd).

Nirenberg, J. (1993) *The Living Organization: Transforming Teams into Workplace Communities* (Homewood, IL: Business One Irwin).

Observer (2010) Interview with David Grossman by Rachel Cooke, 29 August.

Parke, S. (2004) *Church Times*, 25 June.

Phillips, A. (2008) *David: A Story of Passion and Tragedy* (London: SPCK).

Rohr, R. (1993) *Near Occasions of Grace* (New York: Orbis).

Ross, M. (2007) *Pillars of Fire: Power, Priesthood and Spiritual Maturity* (London: Church House Publishing).

Runcorn, D. (1990) *Space for God: Silence and Solitude in the Christian Life* (London: Darton, Longman and Todd).

Runcorn, D. (2002) *Choice, Desire and the Will of God* (London: SPCK).

Runcorn, D. (2008) *The Road to Growth Less Travelled: Spiritual Paths in a Missionary Church* (Cambridge: Grove Books).

Runcorn, D. (2011) *Spirituality Workbook: A Guide for Explorers, Pilgrims and Seekers* (London: SPCK).

Sadgrove, M. (2009) *Wisdom and Leadership* (London: SPCK).

Sanford, J. A. (1985) *King Saul: Tragic Hero* (New York: Paulist Press).

Shelton, P., 'Power, Providence and Personality', unpublished lecture notes on 1 and 2 Samuel.

Storr, A. (1997) *Feet of Clay: A Study of Gurus* (San Francisco: HarperCollins).

Suurmond, J.-J. (1994) *Word and Spirit at Play: Towards a Charismatic Theology* (London: SCM Press).

Thomas, R. S. (1993) *Collected Poems 1945–1990* (London: Dent).

Trible, P. (1978) *God and the Rhetoric of Sexuality* (London: SCM Press).

Trible, P. (1984) *Texts of Terror: Literary-Feminist Readings of Biblical Narratives* (London: SCM Press).

Vanstone, W. H. (1982) *The Stature of Waiting* (London: Darton, Longman and Todd).

Walker, A. (ed.) (1993) *Different Gospels: Christian Orthodoxy and Modern Theologies* (London: SPCK).

Walker, C. M. (2010) unpublished PhD research paper, London School of Theology.

Walker, S. P. (2007–08) *The Undefended Leader Trilogy* (Carlisle: Piquant Editions).

Whyte, D. (1994) *The Heart Aroused: Poetry and the Preservation of the Soul of Corporate America* (New York: Doubleday).

Whyte, D. (2001) *Crossing the Unknown Sea: Work as a Pilgrimage of Identity* (London: Penguin).